the Backroads Bike Book

A dozen scenic rides in and around Lambertville, N.J. and New Hope, Pa.

By Catherine D. Kerr

Third edition

Please ride cautiously! **No** matter how carefully a bicycling route is planned, it is impossible to eliminate all potential hazards or to foresee changes in road conditions. Even on bike paths and back roads, bicycle riding always involves a certain degree of risk.

Bicyclists should observe the usual guidelines for safe cycling, including:

- Wear a helmet.
- Stay to the right and ride single file.
- Take care to avoid road hazards such as potholes.
- Always watch out for cars, even where there doesn't appear to be much traffic.
- Don't go so fast you lose control of your bicycle.
- Yield to pedestrians, especially when riding along mixed-use paths.

ISBN 0-9652733-3-4

© 1998, Catherine D. Kerr.
All rights reserved.

No part of this book may be reproduced by any means without written permission from the publisher.

FREEWHEELING PRESS
P.O. Box 540
Lahaska PA 18931

http://www.voicenet.com/~ckerr
e-mail: ckerr@voicenet.com

Printed in the United States of America

the Back Roads Bike Book

A dozen scenic rides in and around Lambertville, N.J. and New Hope, Pa.

By Catherine D. Kerr

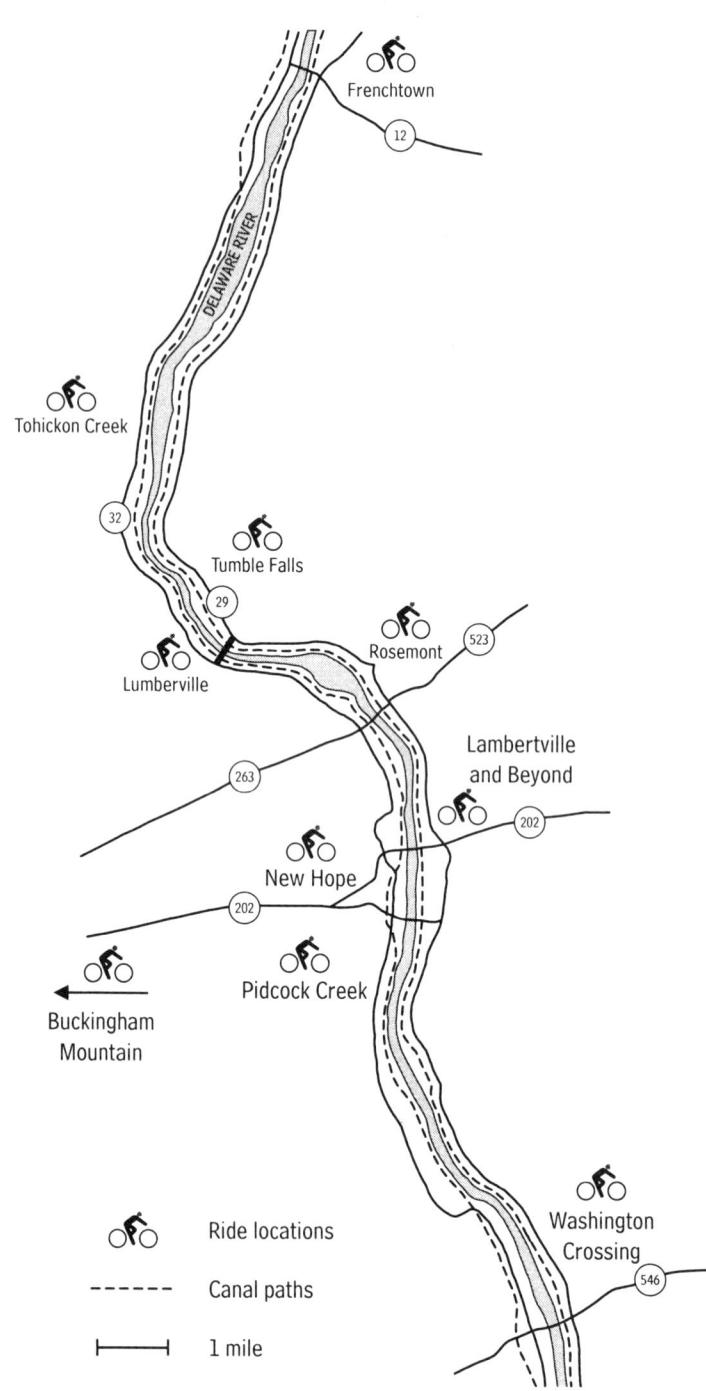

Contents

Introduction vii
New Hope *(9.4 miles)* 1
Lambertville *(9.4 miles)* 7
Beyond Lambertville *(11.4 miles)* 12
Rosemont *(5.9 miles)* 17
Lumberville *(7.4 miles)* 22
Tumble Falls *(11.2 miles)* 27
Tohickon Creek *(10.4 miles)* 31
Frenchtown *(8.8 miles)* 37
Buckingham Mountain *(15.0 miles)* 41
Pidcock Creek *(11.0 miles)* 46
Washington Crossing *(13.4 miles)* 51
Riding the canals 57
Planning longer rides 63
Places to stay 65
Local biking on the Internet 68
Keep in touch 69
Buy a book 70

Thanks!

This book is dedicated to Chris, Nick, and Kate, with thanks for their continuing support of my passion for travel on two wheels and work at my computer.

Many cyclists have helped me over the years in ways that ranged from sharing great biking roads to pointing out that Power Bars become chewable if carried next to the skin. I thank them all.

Introduction

Welcome to the third edition of *The Back Roads Book*!

This new edition includes a stronger cover, improved maps, updated listings, and modifications to a few of the rides, but I've tried to maintain the strengths of the original, which offered a carefully chosen selection of routes showcasing the wonderful scenery near my home in New Hope, Pa., with step-by-step directions, detailed maps, and listings for places to buy refreshments and points of interest along the way.

These rides are designed for people who enjoy leisurely cycling along back roads through woods and farmland where you might not see a car for miles. They will be most appreciated by serious bicyclists looking for an alternative to the 25- to 40-mile routes featured in most bicycle tour books. The shortest of the rides can be accomplished at an unhurried pace in about an hour, though stopping to picnic or dine at an informal restaurant—or to browse the shops in one of the charming little towns along the Delaware River—can turn the outing into an afternoon's pastime. (I have not attempted to estimate times for the rides, knowing that some cyclists may want to pedal straight through while others will be happy to dawdle. If you need to predict how long you'll be gone and you don't know how fast you normally ride, you can figure eight to ten miles an hour as a fairly leisurely pace.)

My suggested routes are planned to avoid monster hills and the busiest roadways. They allow you to ride up more gentle rises and coast down the steeper inclines wherever possible—which is not to say that you won't find any hills at all. The Delaware River is the central geographic feature of this region; from there, everything else is uphill. Routes 29 and 32, which follow the river, are mostly flat, but they tend to be narrow and quite heavily trafficked near Lambertville and New Hope. The only way to avoid hills and cars completely is to limit your riding to the canals that run along the Delaware River. Everything else does occasionally go up and down.

Good maps and clear directions will guide you through every ride. The maps are designed to provide enough information to allow you to make short departures from the planned route or to find your way again if you happen to make a wrong turn, although they don't include every street. In calculating distances, I relied on a combination of car and bicycle odometers and maps. These figures are provided for your guidance but they are estimates only.

The layout of the maps and directions might seem a bit odd, but the sideways design is intended to make it easier to stop and consult these sections while you are on the road. When the cues run to more than one page, the maps are repeated so you can always view both map and directions without having to flip back and forth in the book. Also, cyclists who use the type of handlebar bag that has a clear map case on top should be able to carry the book right in the map case. (Please be sure to stop your bike before studying the directions.)

The book includes listings for places to eat and things to do along each route. These are some of my personal favorites; I haven't tried to provide comprehensive listings for everything you'll pass. The restaurants I've chosen are casual places where bicycling clothing would be acceptable. Some of the restaurants close one day a week, most often on Mondays, so you might want to call ahead to make sure any restaurant you're counting on visiting will be open when you arrive.

There's also a chapter on places to stay near Lambertville and New Hope. Again, this list isn't comprehensive. There are far too many wonderful inns and bed & breakfasts in this area to list them all, but this section should at least give you an idea of what's available.

Please pay careful attention to the safety suggestions listed on the second page of this book. I've tried hard to be selective about which roads to include here, avoiding those with narrow shoulders and lots of traffic, but bicycling always involves a certain degree of risk. (You might never see a car on some of the roads in this book, but if you're really concerned about avoiding automobile traffic, early weekend mornings are probably the best times to ride.)

Adapt your riding to the surface of the road. Back roads by definition are not as well maintained as major thoroughfares. Some of the routes in this book include unpaved roads (as well as some supposedly paved roads that are even rougher). I've tried to include warnings about these areas, but be aware that road conditions can change without warning.

Finally, I wish you all happy cycling—and I hope you have as much fun using this book as I've had putting it together!

                              Catherine D. Kerr

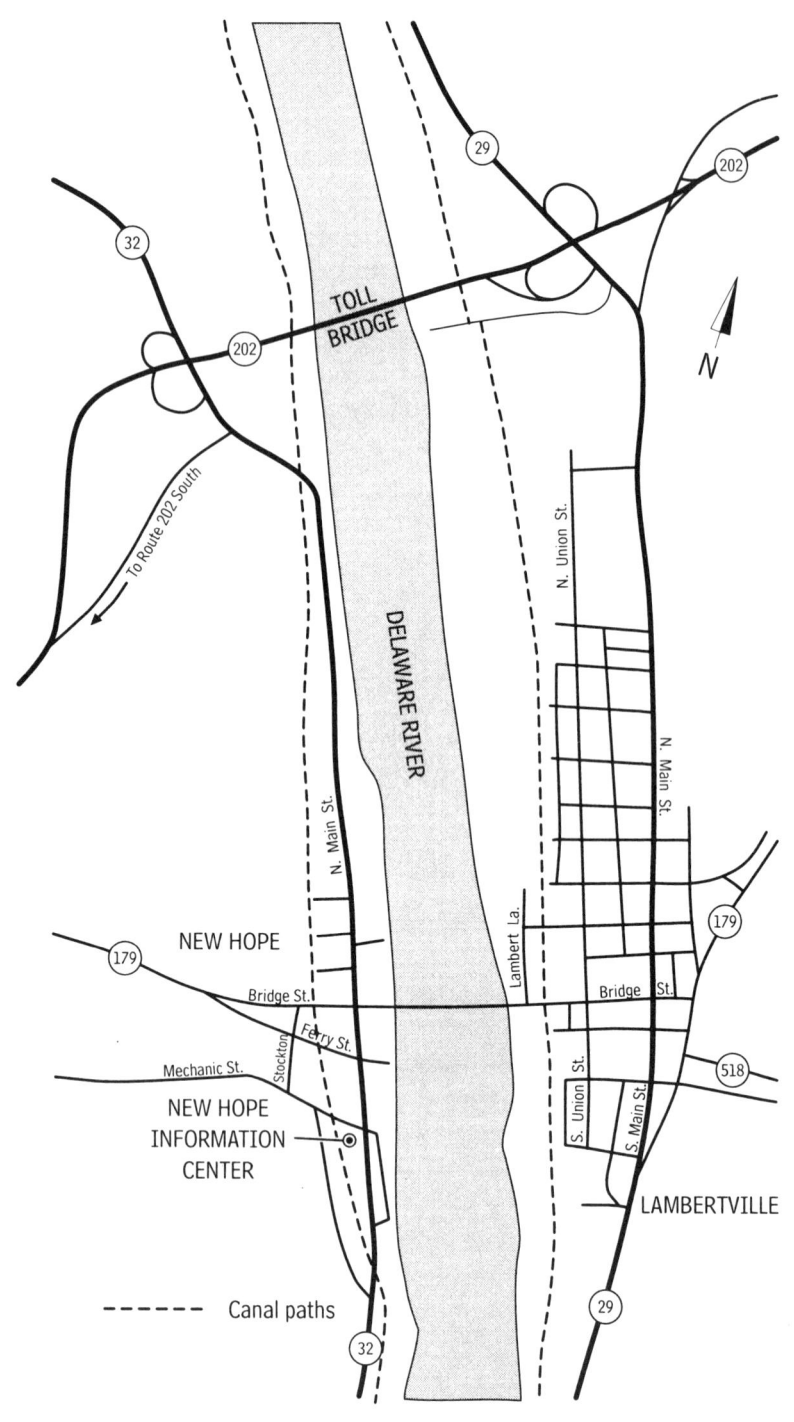

New Hope

Distance: 9.4 miles
Start: New Hope Information Center
           Mechanic St.
           New Hope, Pa.

Bicycling in New Hope? Sure, all those shops and restaurants make it a great place to visit, but is this any place to ride a bike?

If you've seen the town at four on a busy weekend afternoon, when pedestrians clog the sidewalks and spill into the streets and traffic backs up half a mile from the light at Bridge and Main, you might wonder. But drop by first thing in the morning on a fair-weather Saturday or Sunday and it's a different story. Car traffic is down dramatically, pedestrians are few and far between, and the town seems to belong to bicyclists riding through or stopping off at the Village Store for an energy-reviving snack.

Early morning is a fine time for bike riding in New Hope. Parking spaces are plentiful and the meters don't go into effect until 10 A.M., so you can park for free almost anywhere you choose. You can pick a spot near one of the restaurants on Main Street and enjoy a hearty breakfast after your ride, or park near the New Hope Information Center and drop by when you're done to pick up literature and advice on the town's many attractions. For the purpose of keeping track of mileage, this ride officially begins at the information center,

Main Street in New Hope: A popular tourist destination

which is located at the intersection of South Main and Mechanic streets.

Riding west on Mechanic Street, you'll cross the Delaware Canal and pass quickly into the woods surrounding Ingham Creek. Later, as you continue west on Stoney Hill Road, the countryside opens up a little, and it isn't unusual to see song-birds swooping through the fields on a sunny morning. After crossing to the north side of Route 202, you'll glide along Meetinghouse Road through open fields and cool woods to the Solebury Friends Meetinghouse. The last sections of Aquetong and Meetinghouse roads present the most significant uphill climbs on this ride; the rest is either gently uphill or emphatically down.

When you reach River Road (Route 32) again, you'll find Magill's Hill Park, used mostly for sledding in the winter. You can stop to rest there across from the pretty little St. Philip's Episcopal Church before riding back into New Hope.

Good to know:

Although these listings are very short, New Hope is arguably the most interesting town in the area. (Lambertville is a close second.) But writing about every shop and restaurant worth visiting here would require a separate book. If you can spare the time after your ride, walk around and explore for yourself. New Hope's business district is only about a half mile long, and Lambertville is within walking distance via the bridge over the Delaware River. You can obtain detailed information about the town at the New Hope Borough Information Center.

New Hope Borough Information Center, South Main and Mechanic sts., New Hope, (215) 862-5880. Tourist information.

New Hope Cyclery, 186 Old York Rd., New Hope, (215) 862-6888. A small bike shop, a little off the beaten path, which also offers rentals.

The Village Store, 16 S. Main St., New Hope, (215) 862-5485. Take-out coffee, ice cream cones, cold drinks, sandwiches, etc. Popular with the bicycle crowd; opens early.

New Hope

🚴 Start at the New Hope Information Center at the intersection of S. Main and Mechanic sts. Ride west on Mechanic.

0.1 At the stop sign at Stockton Ave., go **straight** ahead to continue on Mechanic.

0.6 Bear **left** onto Stoney Hill Rd. (unmarked) when Mechanic goes to the right.

0.8 After the stop sign, stay to the **right** to continue on Stoney Hill when Sugan Rd. goes off to the left.

2.6 At the stop sign, turn **right** onto Aquetong Rd.

3.6 At the stop sign, cross Route 202 carefully and continue **straight** on Aquetong.

4.3 Turn **right** onto Meetinghouse Rd.

6.1 When Meetinghouse ends at a stop sign, turn **right** onto Sugan.

6.7	Turn **left** onto Chapel Rd. (The curve ahead in Sugan makes it hard to see oncoming traffic, so turn carefully.)
7.8	At the stop sign, turn **right** onto River Rd. (The sign here also says Route 32 in small letters.)
8.2	Ride under Route 202. (Be very careful here because there may be traffic getting on and off the highway.)
8.4	Cross the Delaware Canal on a small bridge; the road curves sharply here.
9.4	Return to the New Hope Information Center.

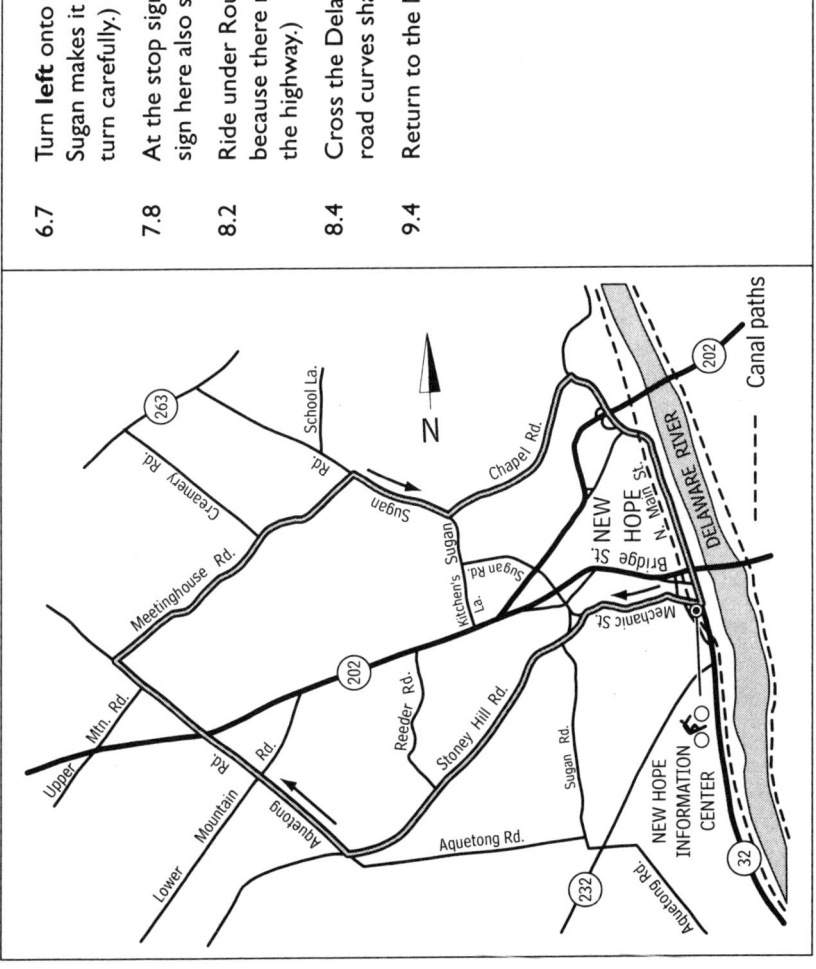

New Hope ◆ 5

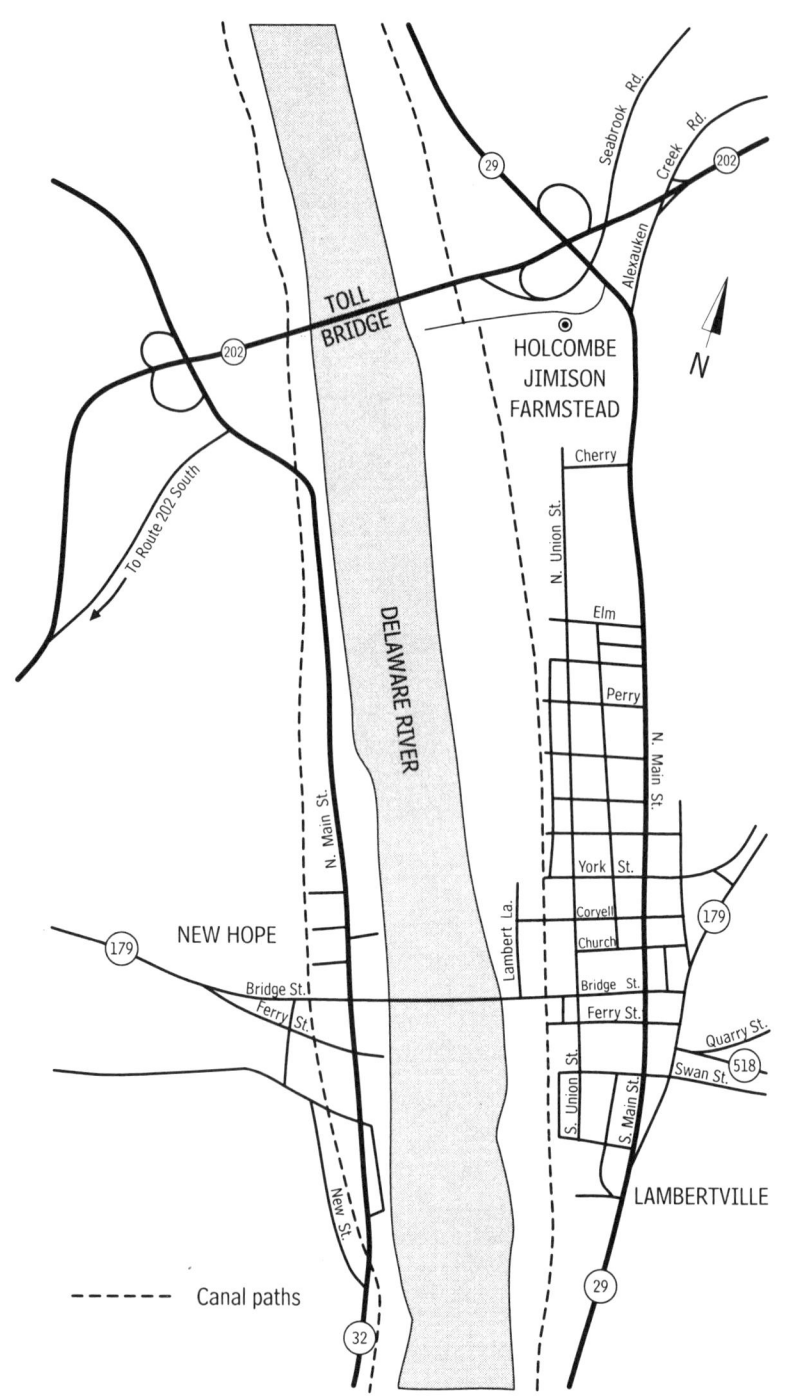

Lambertville

Distance: 9.4 miles
Start: Parking lot behind Holcombe Jimison Farmstead Lambertville, N.J.

Lambertville is a city of contrasts. A nineteenth-century manufacturing center, it is currently enjoying a renaissance as a tourist destination. Its restaurants, antiques shops, booksellers, and coffee houses are popular with out-of-town visitors, especially on weekends.

This is a quaint little city with a history, and the central district has a pleasantly old-fashioned urban ambience, yet just beyond the city limits lie farms and woodlands that beckon to bike riders with a yen for the open road.

In the center of Lambertville, Bridge and North Union streets are the focus of commercial activity, but you'll also find interesting shops on some of the side streets such as Lambert Lane or Coryell Street. The Delaware & Raritan Canal flows under Bridge Street next to the Lambertville Station (now a restaurant, not a train depot). From here you can get on the canal bike path and ride south through Washington Crossing almost to Trenton or north to Frenchtown. A long-awaited construction project completed in the summer of 1998 made it possible to cycle straight through Lambertville on the path. (See page 57 for detailed information about riding along the canal.)

One thing the center of Lambertville does not have a lot of is parking, and most of what you will find is metered. For that reason, this ride begins at the north end of the city in a parking lot located right next to the Route 202 toll bridge over the Delaware River. To find the lot from Route 29, turn at the sign for the Holcombe Jimison Farmstead Museum. (It's just south of Route 202.) Drive past the farm buildings on your left and continue down to the parking area next to the canal.

You'll begin this ride by taking your bike back up to Route 29. At the sign for the Holcombe Jimison Farmstead Museum, turn right onto Route 29. Cars and trucks travel fast on this short four-lane stretch of roadway, but there is room for bikes if you are cautious. Be especially careful crossing Route 29 to make the left turn at Alexauken Creek Road, which is also marked by a sign for northbound Route 202.

Alexauken Creek Road quickly brings you into the countryside, but you will want to take special care again when you pass the on and off ramps for Route 202. After that, the road follows the creek as you make a steady but mostly gentle climb out of the river valley.

The rest of this ride is quite rural. There's a hill to climb on Sandy Ridge-Mount Airy Road as you approach the intersection with Lambertville-Headquarters Road. On Buchanan Road, you'll pass Sarah Dilts Farm, a Delaware Township park with sports fields, picnic areas, and rest rooms.

Toward the end of the ride, when Seabrook Road meets Lambertville-Headquarters Road, there's a sweeping view of the river valley, with Lambertville and New Hope visible in the distance. From here it's all downhill back to Route 29.

There are no shops or restaurants directly on the route, so you might want to bring a picnic lunch, or you can stop for refreshments in Lambertville at the end of the ride. To get to the center of town, pick up the canal path near the parking area where you left your car and ride south for about a mile.

Good to know:

Mountain River Outfitters, 287 S. Main St., Lambertville, (609) 397-3366. A variety of outdoor offerings, including bicycle rentals.

Giuseppe's Pizzeria, 40 Bridge St., Lambertville, (609) 397-1500. The primary virtues of Giuseppe's are easy to summarize: It has pizza, and it's there.

Holcombe Jimison Farmstead Museum, Route 29, Lambertville, (609) 397-2752. Blacksmith shop and a collection of farm buildings and equipment dedicated to preserving Hunterdon County's rural heritage. Usually open weekends only.

Lambertville Fine Food & Flowers, Bridge and Main sts., Lambertville, (609) 397-4040. Sandwiches to go, cold drinks, coffee, etc.

Lambertville Trading Company, 43 Bridge St., Lambertville, (609) 397-2232. Coffee, cappuccino, pastries, etc., with lots of atmosphere.

Wheel Fine Bicycle Shop, 639 Brunswick Pike (Route 518), West Amwell Township, (609) 397-3403. A small but well-stocked bike shop about 2.5 miles from Lambertville on the road to Hopewell.

Lambertville

🚲 Start at Route 29 next to the sign for the Holcombe Jimison Farmstead Museum. Turn **right** onto Route 29. (**Be very careful** on this short stretch of four-lane roadway.) Cross Alexauken Creek and immediately turn **left** onto Alexauken Creek Rd. (Alexauken Creek Rd. is also marked by signs for northbound Route 202.)

0.2 Continue **straight** on Alexauken when it passes under Route 202. Watch out for traffic using the on and off ramps for the highway.

2.4 When Alexauken ends at a stop sign, turn **left** onto Queen Rd. (It becomes Sandy Ridge-Mt. Airy Rd.)

3.4 Turn **right** onto Lambertville-Headquarters Rd.

4.1 Turn **left** onto Buchanan Rd.

4.6 Pass Sarah Dilts Farm on your **right**.

4.9 At the stop sign, turn **left** onto Sandy Ridge Rd.

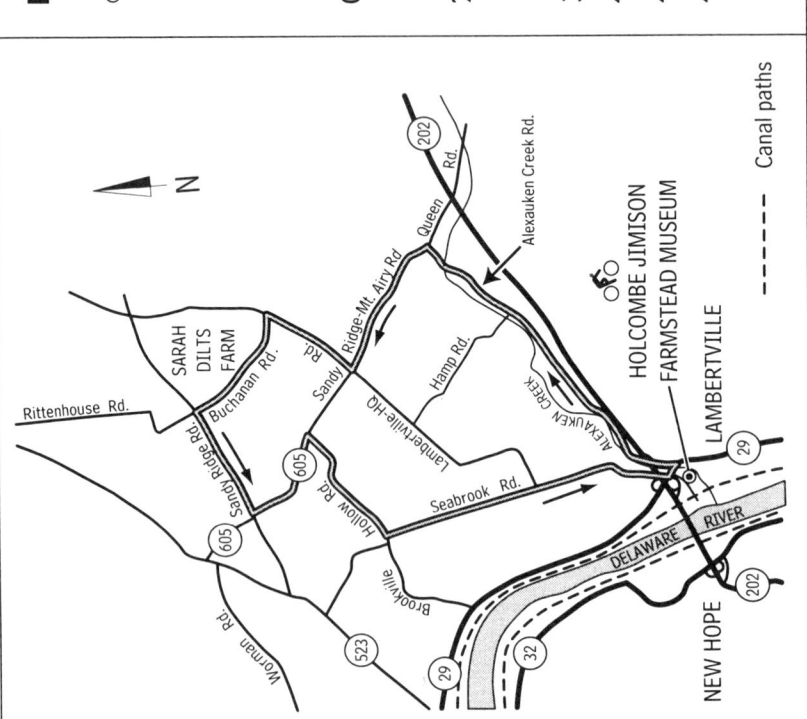

5.7 At the Sandy Ridge Church, turn **left** onto Sandy Ridge-Mt. Airy Rd.

6.4 Turn **right** onto Brookville Hollow Rd.

7.3 Turn **left** onto Seabrook Rd.

8.4 At the stop sign, go **straight** to continue on Lambertville-Headquarters.

9.4 When Lambertville-Headquarters ends at a stop sign at Route 29, **cross** the four lanes carefully, turn **left** and cross the railroad tracks, then immediately turn **right** at the Holcombe Jimison Farmstead sign to return to the parking area.

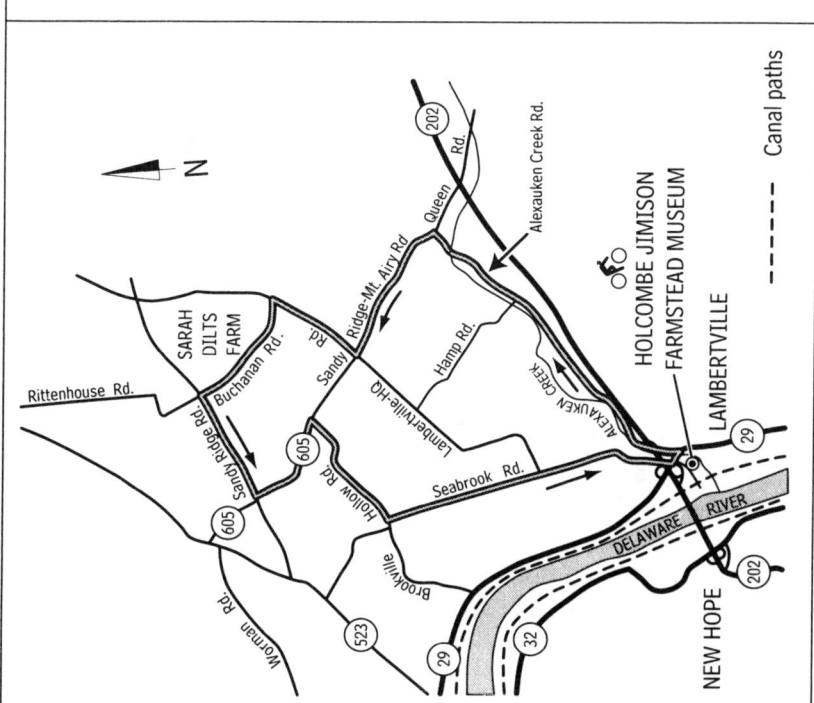

Beyond Lambertville

Distance: 11.4 miles
Start: Sarah Dilts Farm
            Buchanan Rd.
            Delaware Township, N.J.

Some of the best bicycling back roads in the area can be found just beyond the bustling little city of Lambertville. You may find it hard to believe that you're never far from civilization on this ride, which travels through a rural landscape dotted with big barns and quaint country churches.

Sarah Dilts Farm, the starting point, is a Delaware Township park best known locally for its soccer and baseball fields. It also has picnic areas, rest rooms, a playground, and plenty of parking. It's a big park, but when no sports events are scheduled, there's often no one there at all.

The first part of the ride is relatively flat. It takes you past cornfields to the outskirts of the crossroads town of Sergeantsville. A blinking red light at the intersection of Rosemont-Ringoes Road and Route 523 is a sign that there is more traffic here than on most of the roads on this ride, but Sergeantsville is certainly not a major center of commerce. It does boast one place where you can stop for refreshments: The Sergeantsville General Store, located about a tenth of a mile off the planned route. Since there are no other shops or restaurants on the ride, you might want to visit this store, which sells sandwiches and other takeout food. To reach it, turn left instead of right when Rittenhouse Road ends at Rosemont-Ringoes Road in Sergeantsville. You'll find the Sergeantsville General Store on the far right at the corner of Route 523.

From Sergeantsville, you'll ride out past the Amwell Church of the Brethren and through the woods to the tracks of the Black River & Western Railroad. The route follows the railroad for a while before heading back toward Sarah Dilts Farm. From Sergeantsville on, the terrain becomes a little more challenging, and you'll climb hills on Rosemont-Ringoes, Boss, Bowne Station, and Sandy Ridge-Mount Airy roads.

Good to know:

Sergeantsville General Store, Rosemont-Ringoes Rd., Sergeantsville, (609) 397-3214. Cold drinks and takeout foods in a country store that welcomes cyclists.

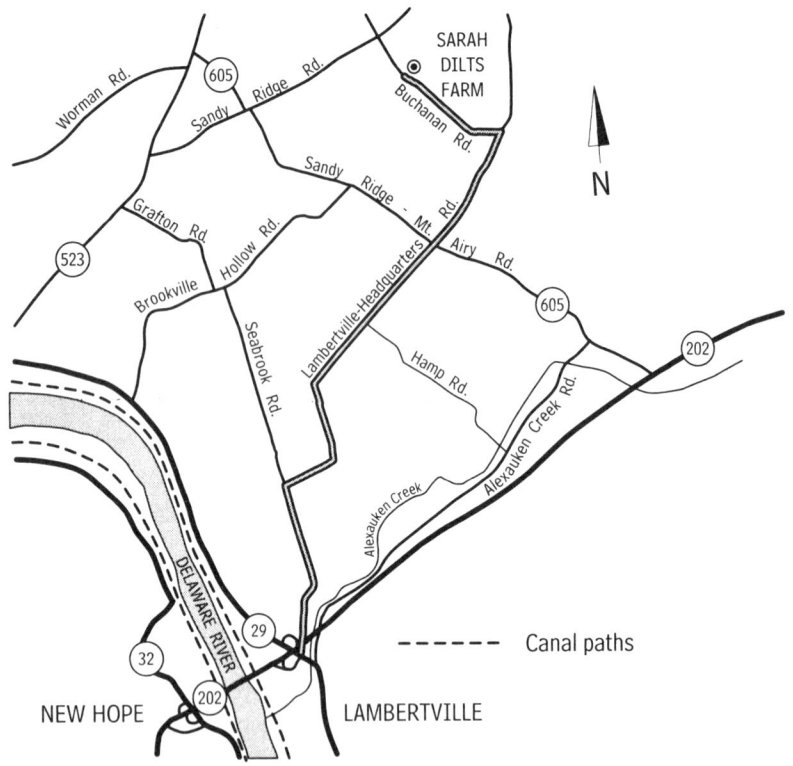

Finding Sarah Dilts Farm

Sarah Dilts Farm is only four miles from Route 29 in Lambertville, but finding it can be tricky. Seabrook Road, the turnoff, is just north of the railroad tracks that cross Route 29; it is directly across from the exit ramp leading from the northbound lanes of Route 202. It is marked with a small green sign pointing to Headquarters; there are also signs for both Seabrook Road and Lambertville-Headquarters Road.

0.0   Turn from Route 29 onto Seabrook Rd.
0.9   Turn right onto Lambertville-Headquarters Rd.
2.7   At the stop sign, go straight to continue on Lambertville-Headquarters.
3.4   Turn left onto Buchanan Rd.
4.0   Turn right into Sarah Dilts Farm.

Beyond Lambertville

🚲 Start at Sarah Dilts Farm. Turn **right** onto Buchanan Rd.

0.3 At the stop sign at Sandy Ridge Rd., go **straight** to continue on Rittenhouse Rd.

1.7 When Rittenhouse ends at a stop sign, turn **right** onto Rosemont-Ringoes Rd. (which isn't marked).

2.1 At the end of the Delaware Township School property, bear **left** onto Lambert Rd. (Follow the sign for the Amwell Church of the Brethren.)

3.3 When Lambert ends at a stop sign (the Church of the Brethren will be straight ahead), turn **right** onto Sandbrook-Headquarters Rd. You will cross a stream and immediately turn **left** onto Dunkard Church Rd.

4.3 Turn **right** onto Haines Rd.

5.0 When Haines ends at a stop sign, turn **left** onto Rosemont-Ringoes.

5.6 Turn **right** onto Boss Rd.

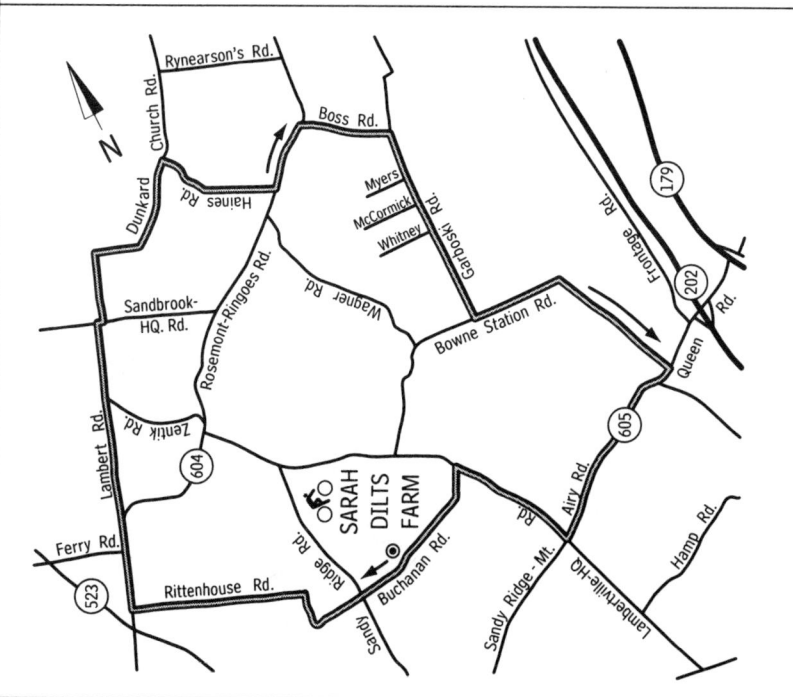

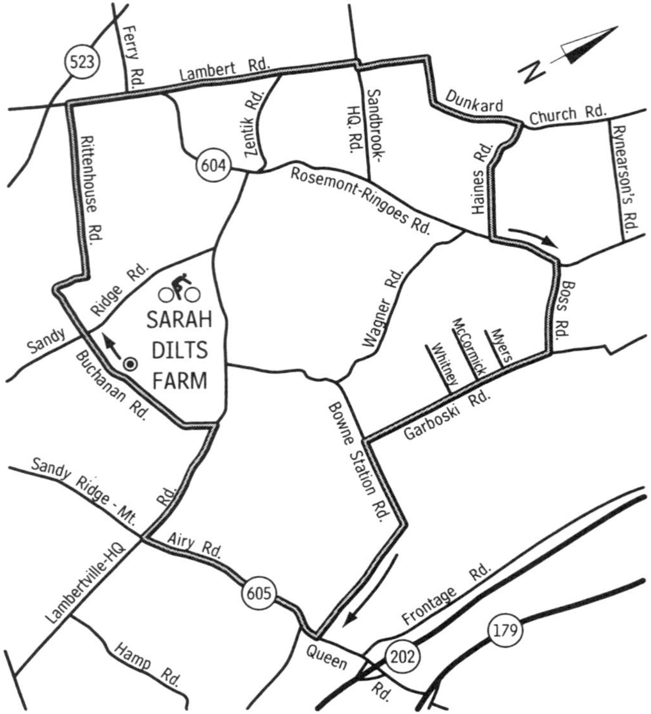

6.2 Just before the railroad tracks, turn **right** onto Garboski Rd.

7.9 When Garboski ends at a stop sign, turn **left** onto Bowne Station Rd.

9.2 When Bowne Station ends at a stop sign, turn **right** onto a road marked Queen Rd. (It becomes Sandy Ridge-Mount Airy.)

10.2 Turn **right** onto Lambertville-Headquarters Rd.

11.0 Turn **left** onto Buchanan.

11.4 Return to Sarah Dilts Farm.

16 ◆ *The Back Roads Bike Book*

Rosemont

Distance: 5.9 miles
Start: Prallsville Mills
Route 29
Stockton, N.J.

The route from Stockton to Rosemont and back is one of the shortest, easiest, and prettiest rides in this book.

The ride starts on Route 29 about a half mile north of Bridge Street in Stockton at Prallsville Mills, a collection of restored buildings that housed a sawmill, grist mill, and linseed oil mill in the eighteenth and nineteenth centuries. The site includes ample parking, a great view of the Delaware River, and easy access to the path that runs next to the Delaware & Raritan Canal. (See page 57 for more information on biking the canal.)

After a very short ride on Route 29, you'll turn onto Route 519 and then onto Lower Creek Road, which follows the Wickecheoke Creek all the way to the last remaining historic covered bridge in New Jersey. On the way, the creek burbles along through the protected woodlands of the Wickecheoke Reserve, which has been dedicated as a permanent conservation area. The road along the creek goes ever so slightly uphill, the rise so gentle you may not even notice it.

After Green Sergeant's Covered Bridge, which was built in 1866, you'll hit the only serious uphill on the ride. When you reach the sign

Two of the historic buildings at Prallsville Mills

that says "Hunterdon County Route 604, 1 mile," the worst is over. The payoff: A sweeping view of open farmland, with cornfields on the left and cows grazing on the right, and a quick pass through the tiny village of Rosemont, where you can stop for lunch at The Cafe, a restaurant with a cozy ambience to match the tenor of the town. Leaving Rosemont, you'll make short work of the downhill on Route 519, which brings you back to Route 29 and the mill.

As an alternative to avoid the hills entirely, ride out along the Wickecheoke Creek to the covered bridge and back the same way.

At the end of the ride, you can pick up the canal path behind the mill and ride into the town of Stockton, where you can stop to eat at Meil's Restaurant and Bakery. Dilly's Corner, a good place to get a hamburger or an ice cream cone, is in Centre Bridge just across the Delaware River from Stockton.

Good to know:

The Cafe, Routes 519 and 604, Rosemont, (609) 397-4097. Friendly and informal; a great place to stop for lunch on the ride.

Cravings, 10 Risler St. (Route 29), Stockton (609) 397-2911. A very basic burgers and ice cream sort of place with both indoor and outdoor seating, located about a quarter-mile south of Prallsville Mills.

Dilly's Corner, Routes 263 and 32, Centre Bridge, (215) 862-5333. A classic hamburger and ice cream stand just across the bridge over the Delaware from Stockton.

Meil's Restaurant and Bakery, Bridge and Main sts., Stockton, (609) 397-8033. Great food and desserts in a casual atmosphere.

Rosemont

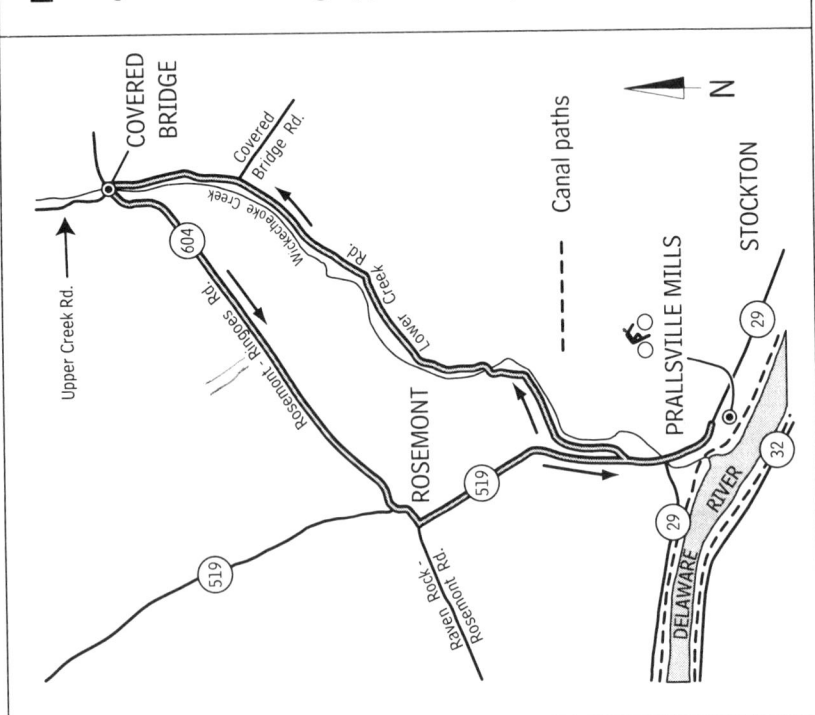

🚲 Start at Prallsville Mills. Turn **left** from the northern driveway of the mill property onto Route 29; immediately cross the Wickecheoke Creek and stay **straight** to proceed on Route 519 (Kingwood-Stockton Rd.). (Route 29 goes off to the left.)

0.2 Turn **right** onto Lower Creek Rd.

2.8 When Lower Creek Rd. ends at a stop sign, turn **left** onto Rosemont-Ringoes Rd. (Route 604); ride through the covered bridge and continue **straight** on Route 604.

4.7 When Rosemont-Ringoes ends at a stop sign, turn **left** onto Route 519. (Just after this turn, 519 curves sharply to the right.)

4.8 Turn **left** to continue on Route 519. (Raven Rock Rd. goes straight ahead.)

20 ◆ The Back Roads Bike Book

5.9 When Route 519 ends at a stop sign, go **straight** to proceed on Route 29 and immediately cross the Wickecheoke Creek. At the end of the bridge over the creek, turn **right** into the Prallsville Mills parking area.

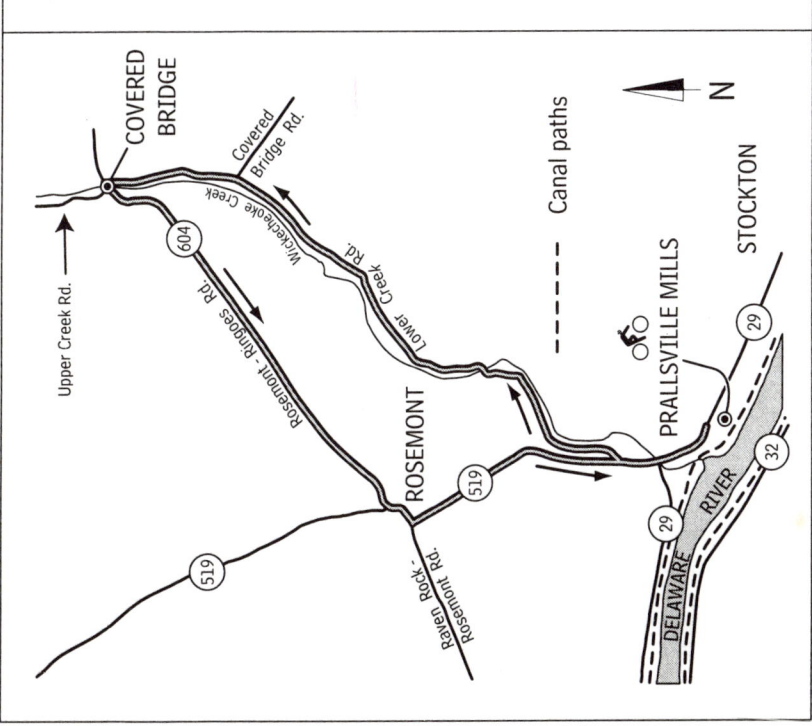

Lumberville

Distance: 7.4 miles
Start: Lock No. 12
River Road (Route 32)
Lumberville, Pa.

This little gem of a ride starts in Lumberville, a quiet river town of Victorian frame houses located on the bank of the Delaware River about six miles north of New Hope. A pedestrian bridge joins the town with the Bull's Island Recreation Area in New Jersey, which has parking and picnic areas and an easy path down to the river. You might find it easier to leave your car there and walk your bike across to Lumberville, but wherever you park, you should definitely take a stroll out across the river just to admire the view.

From Lumberville, the route goes up to the town of Carversville and back down again on roads that follow the Paunnacussing and Cuttalossa creeks. Although the ride to Carversville is definitely uphill, narrow Fleecydale Road provides a very gradual climb, and the road is closed to all but local traffic much of the way. Cuttalossa Road, the downhill route, rolls through woods and past a beautiful little farm. It's unpaved part of the way and doesn't really go anywhere, so it, too, carries very little traffic.

The route does use short stretches of Sugan Road and Route 32, which are more heavily traveled than the rest of the ride. There should not be a lot of traffic on Route 32, but what there is will go

Cuttalossa Road: One of the prettiest places in Bucks County

fast. If this makes you uncomfortable, there is an alternative: Turn right when Cuttalossa Road ends at Route 32, then left to cross the Delaware Canal at the quarry; follow the towpath back to Lumberville, where you can come back across the canal on a bridge near the beginning of the ride. Although you will avoid the traffic this way, the towpath can be bumpy.

Another alternative for a short but extremely pleasant ride is to travel up to Carversville and back along Fleecydale Road. (Don't be tempted to make a loop ride out of Fleecydale and Old Carversville roads unless you're a glutton for tough hills and rough road.) Even if you don't ride back along the towpath, you can use the bridge over the canal at Lock No. 12 in Lumberville to cross over to a group of picnic tables in a nice spot beside the river.

Both Lumberville and Carversville are primarily residential towns, but each has a store selling food to go, so you can stock up before you start your ride, take a break for refreshment halfway through, or buy a takeout lunch and enjoy it and the view of the river when you are done.

Good to know:

Lumberville Store & Gallery, River Rd., Lumberville, (215) 297-5388. Food to go, arts and crafts, books, and bicycle rentals. A very nice place to end your ride.

Carversville General Store, Aquetong and Fleecydale rds., Carversville, (215) 297-5353. A real old-fashioned country store. It is home to the Carversville Post Office and offers everything from tools to groceries. The store also sells sandwiches and cold drinks, and there's a bench and a bike rack outside.

Bull's Island Recreation Area, 2185 Daniel Bray Highway (Route 29), Stockton, N.J. 08559, (609)-397-2949. This 80-acre park on the Delaware River about three miles north of the town of Stockton is located at the very beginning of the Delaware & Raritan Canal. It has areas for picnicking, launching canoes, and camping. A pedestrian bridge connects the park with the town of Lumberville, Pa.

Lumberville

- 🚴 Start on Route 32 (River Rd.) at the sign for Lock No. 12 of the Delaware Canal, just north of the pedestrian bridge over the river. Ride north on Route 32.

- 0.1 At the end of the bridge over Paunnacussing Creek, turn **left** onto Fleecydale Rd. There are signs announcing that the road is open only to local traffic, but bicycles can pass easily.

- 2.2 At the stop sign next to the Carversville Inn, bear **left** onto Aquetong Rd.

- 2.7 Turn **left** onto Sawmill Rd.

- 3.7 When Sawmill ends, turn **right** onto Sugan Rd.

- 4.1 At the stop sign at Greenhill Rd., go **straight** to continue on Sugan.

- 4.7 At the stop sign at Mechanicsville Rd., turn **left** to continue on Sugan.

- 4.9 After crossing a one-lane stone bridge, immediately bear **left** onto Cuttalossa Rd.

Lumberville ◆ 25

6.4 When Cuttalossa ends at a stop sign, turn **left** onto River Rd. (Route 32).

7.4 Return to Lock No. 12.

Tumble Falls

Distance: 11.2 miles
Start: Bull's Island Recreation Area
Route 29
Delaware Township, N.J.

This ride passes varied scenery, from the flatlands along the Delaware River to farms and woods high above, but its most impressive feature is the series of waterfalls next to Route 29 between the Bull's Island Recreation Area and Warsaw Road.

Along this part of the river, steep cliffs rise sharply from Route 29, and you'll pass waterfalls large and small as you ride along. Strictly speaking, Tumble Falls is an area above the falls you'll be passing, but the name is a good description for all of these streams. When you turn onto Warsaw Road, you'll ride for a mile and a half along a creek bed cut out of rock that has been carved into massive boulders in some places and laid out in smooth sheets in others. The lower part of the stream is a continuous rocky waterfall.

Be warned, however: Though this ride is beautiful, it is also more challenging than most of the others in this book. The first half mile of Warsaw Road is a steep climb, and the rest of Warsaw is steadily uphill.

The ride begins at the Bull's Island Recreation Area, about seven miles north of Lambertville. You can start by riding on the Delaware & Raritan bike path, or on the wide, smooth shoulder along Route

29. The path is shaded and very pleasant here, but if you take it you'll miss a very nice waterfall next to Route 29—although there will still be more falls to come. If you do take the path, you must cross over to Route 29 when the two run side by side about a mile and a half north of the park; if you don't, you won't be able to make the turn onto Warsaw Road.

The first little section of Warsaw is the steepest part of the ride. As you continue uphill on Warsaw, the road follows a stream bed and the land is wooded until you reach a (somewhat aromatic) dairy farm at Barbertown-Idell Road. Later, woods and farms will alternate as you ride along the rolling hills of winding Federal Twist Road.

After Warsaw, the rest of the ride is either flat or downhill. The last mile or so of Federal Twist Road is a steep downhill, with a nice view looking across the Delaware River to the Pennsylvania hills just before the road ends at Route 29. From here, it's about a half mile back to Bull's Island.

There are no stores on restaurants on this ride; see the listings for Lumberville on page 22 and Rosemont on page 17 for nearby establishments.

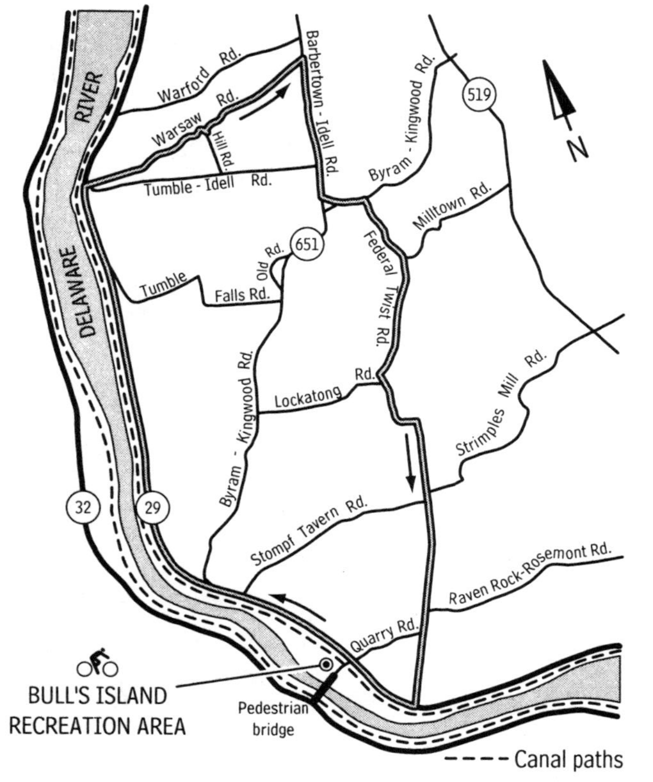

Tumble Falls

🚴 Start at the Bull's Island Recreation Area. At the stop sign where the park road intersects Route 29, turn **left** to head north along Route 29. (You can take the road or the bike path.)

1.8 If you're on the bike path, cross over to Route 29 at the third set of gates across the path and ride on the shoulder of the road.

4.2 Turn **right** onto Warsaw Rd.

5.1 Just after the second bridge carrying Warsaw over the creek, turn **left** to continue on Warsaw. (Hill Rd. goes straight ahead.)

6.0 When Warsaw ends at a stop sign, turn **right** onto Barbertown-Idell Rd. (Route 651).

7.0 At the stop sign, turn **left** onto Byram-Kingwood Rd.

7.3 Turn **right** onto Federal Twist Rd.

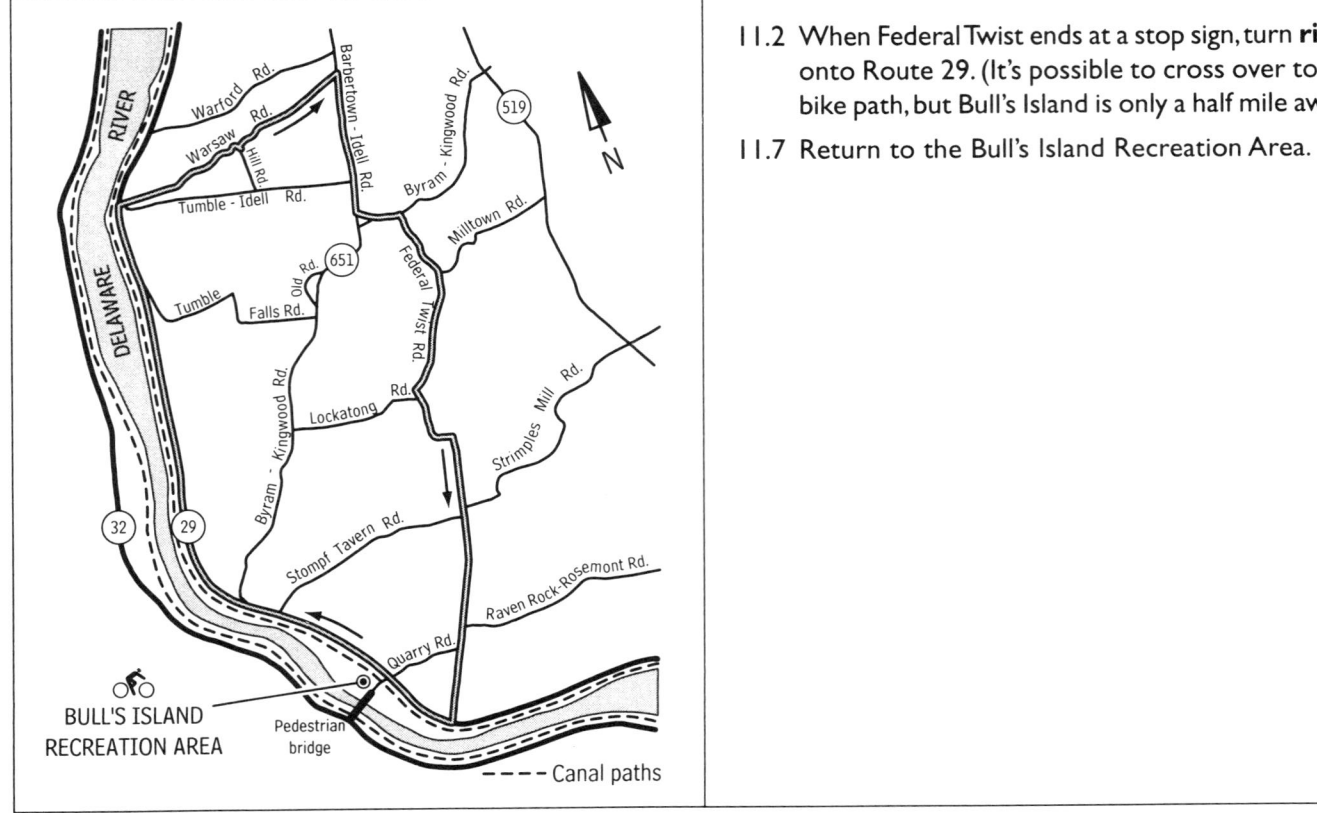

11.2 When Federal Twist ends at a stop sign, turn **right** onto Route 29. (It's possible to cross over to the bike path, but Bull's Island is only a half mile away.)

11.7 Return to the Bull's Island Recreation Area.

Tohickon Creek

Distance: 10.4 miles
Start: Stover-Myers Mill
Dark Hollow Rd.
Pipersville, Pa.

The highlight of this ride is the stunning view from High Rocks Vista in Ralph Stover State Park. From atop a sheer cliff you can look down to Tohickon Creek 200 feet below, or gaze out across a leafy canopy stretching ahead as far as you can see. You'll have the unusual experience of looking down on the birds that fly by, and, if you're not the rock-climbing type, your stomach will do somersaults as you watch the intrepid climbers who flock to this park.

The ride begins at creek level at the Stover-Myers Mill, built around 1800 and now a county park with picnic tables, parking, and rest rooms. At first you will ride on Dark Hollow Road following Tohickon Creek, but you'll soon leave the stream behind and begin the climb toward High Rocks. The ascent is steadily uphill, though generally gradual rather than steep. The first quarter mile on Wormansville Road is the worst hill you'll encounter on your way to High Rocks.

At High Rocks, you can park your bike and walk down through the trees to the edge of the cliff, where the view is just tremendous. When you're ready to ride again, you will take Stover Park Road to Iron Bridge Road, which has a view looking down on Christ Lutheran Church and the buildings around it. From there you'll head out into

The Cabin Run Covered Bridge, built in 1871

more rolling countryside, returning finally to Dark Hollow Road and the parking area near the mill.

Some of the roads on the route are paved and others are not, but you should be prepared for some rough riding on both surfaces. Randts Mill Road in particular can be soft and muddy after a good rain; the rest of the time, its unpaved surface tends to be bumpy. Some of the supposedly paved roads can also be quite uneven, depending when the repaving crews last passed by.

A couple of detours from the mapped-out route are worth mentioning.

The first is Stover Park Road. If you turn left at the end of Tory Road after High Rocks Vista, you can follow Stover Park down to a wooden bridge over Tohickon Creek. This is a very pretty spot, but Stover Park Road is quite steep going down to it. You'll have a very hard climb back up if you choose to go that way.

If you want a shorter ride, skip the turn from Stover Park Road onto Iron Bridge Road. Instead, take Stover Park all the way to Dark Hollow, turn left, and retrace your route back to the parking area. This shorter alternative totals 4.6 miles.

If you do ride ahead to Gruver Road, you'll find a lovely farm and a nice stone bridge over Tohickon Creek if you continue just past the turn onto Randts Mill Road. This detour takes you only a little bit out of the way, and the view is worth it.

Finally, for a pleasant cool-down ride after your return to Stover-Myers Mill, you can continue past the parking area on Covered Bridge Road. The road follows the creek for about half a mile to the Cabin Run Covered Bridge, built in 1871. Covered Bridge Road turns uphill after the bridge. You can ride through the bridge and continue as far as you like, then turn around and retrace your route back to the parking area at the mill.

Stover-Myers Mill is about four miles from Point Pleasant, which is about eight and a half miles north of New Hope. There are no stores or restaurants of any kind on this ride, but if you bring supplies for a picnic there are lovely places to enjoy it at the mill or at nearby Ralph Stover State Park. You can stop on your way to pick something up at the Lumberville Store (see the listings for Lumberville on page 22) or at the Point Pleasant Village Store. To reach the parking and picnic areas along Tohickon Creek in the state park after your bike ride, drive along Covered Bridge Road from the Stover-Myers Mill and turn left at Stump Road.

Good to know:

Point Pleasant Village Store, Route 32, Point Pleasant, (215) 297-8124. Cold drinks and sandwiches are on the menu at this store on Route 32 in Point Pleasant; you'll find it just north of the intersection with Point Pleasant Pike.

Bucks County River Country, Walters Lane (just off Route 32), Point Pleasant, (215) 297-5000. The place to go if you want to top off your bike ride with a canoe or tubing trip down the Delaware River.

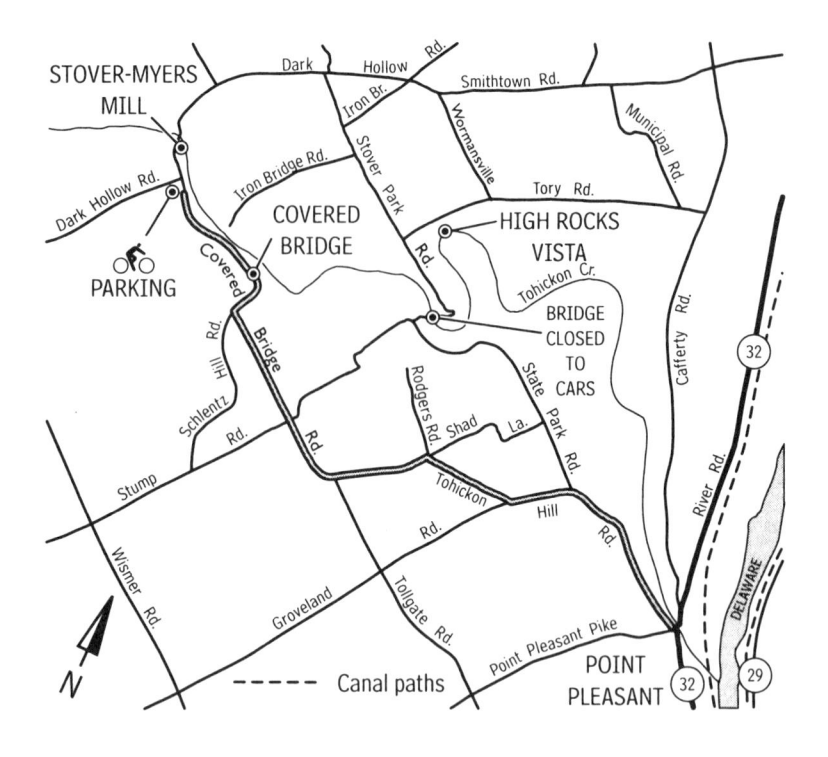

Finding the Stover-Myers Mill

0.0   From the intersection of Route 32 (River Road) and Point Pleasant Pike: Heading north on Route 32, cross Point Pleasant Pike at the stop sign and continue **straight** on Tohickon Hill Rd.

0.9   Continue **straight** on Tohickon Hill Rd. when State Park Rd. goes off to the right.

1.1   Turn **right** to continue on Tohickon Hill Rd. when Groveland Rd. goes off to the left.

1.6   Continue **straight** on Tohickon Hill Rd. when Shad La. and Rodgers Rd. go off to the right.

2.4   Continue **straight** after the stop sign when Tohickon Hill Rd. becomes Covered Bridge Rd.

3.0   Turn **right** at the stop sign to continue on Covered Bridge Rd. (Don't worry if the sign says Schlentz Hill Rd.)

3.8   Turn **left** into the parking area for the mill.

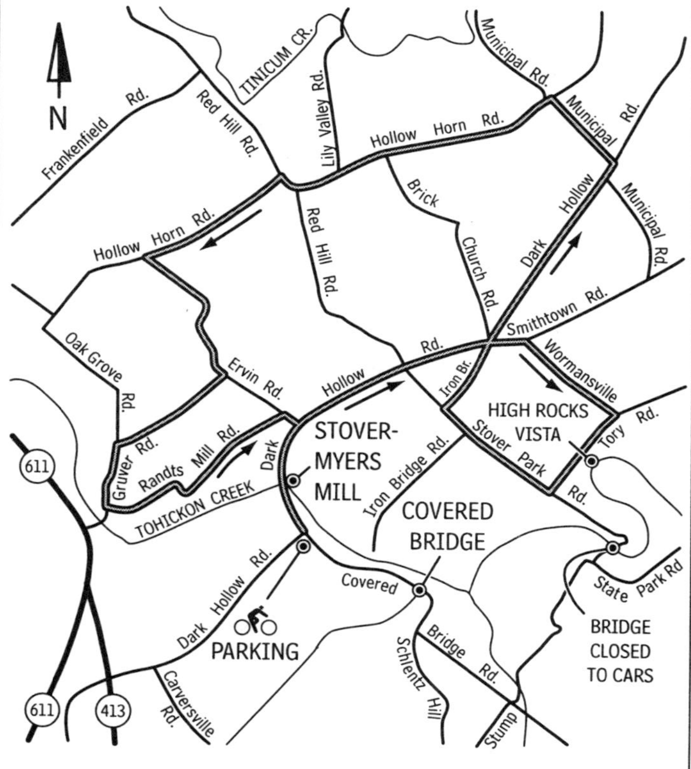

Tohickon Creek

🚲 Start on Covered Bridge Road at the parking lot for the Stover-Myers Mill. Turn **left** out of the parking area and ride toward the mill, going **straight** at the stop sign to continue on Dark Hollow Rd.

1.4 Just after Christ Lutheran Church, go **straight** onto Smithtown Rd. (Dark Hollow goes off to the left; Iron Bridge Rd. goes off to the right.)

1.6 Turn **right** onto Wormansville Rd.

2.1 Turn **right** onto Tory Rd.

2.4 Stop at High Rocks Vista, located to the **left**.

2.6 Turn **right** onto Stover Park Rd.

3.2 Turn **right** onto Iron Bridge Rd.

3.6 At the stop sign at the five-way intersection, go **straight** to continue on Dark Hollow.

4.6 Turn **left** onto Municipal Rd.

5.0 When Municipal Rd. ends at a stop sign, turn **left** onto Hollow Horn Rd.

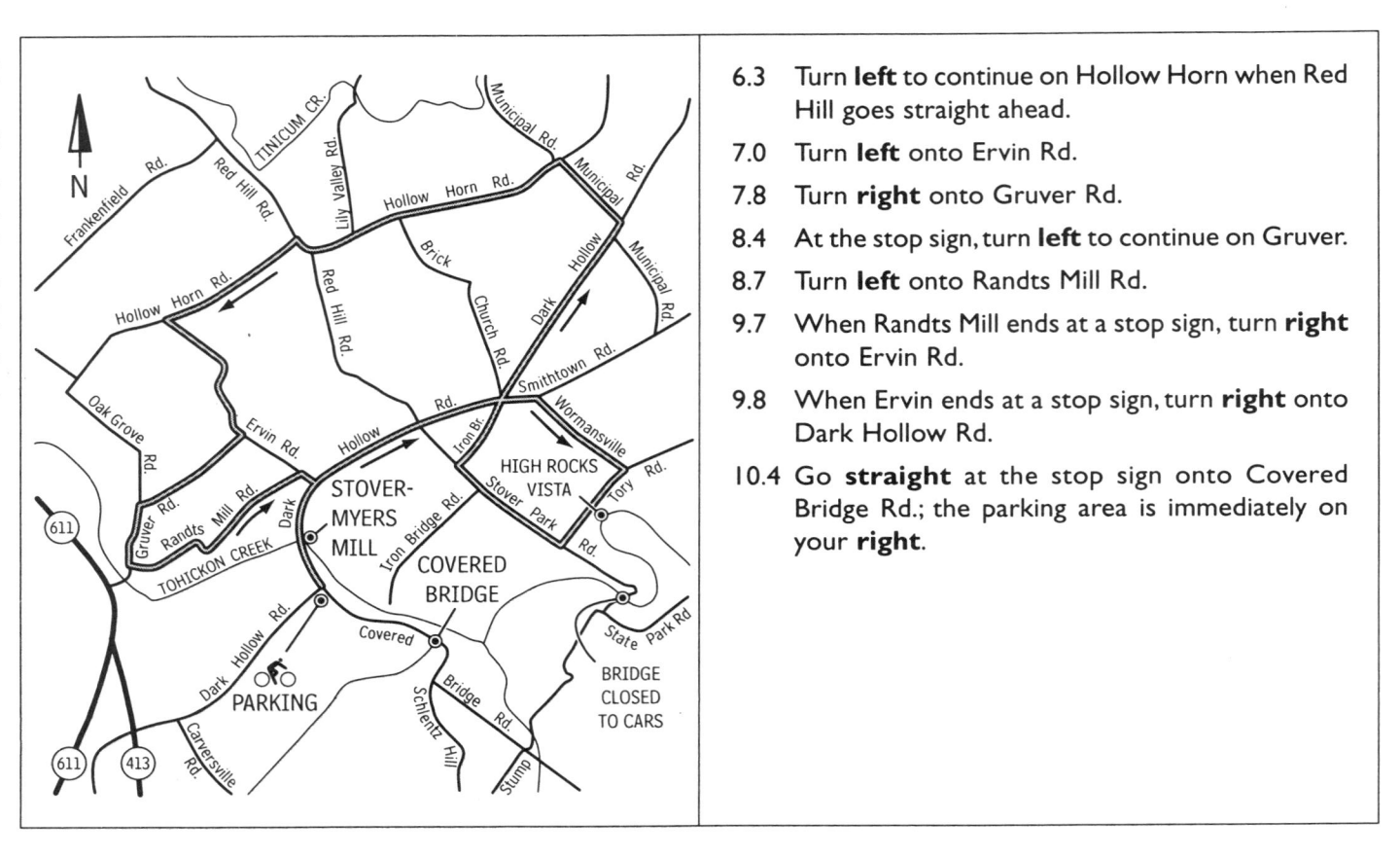

6.3	Turn **left** to continue on Hollow Horn when Red Hill goes straight ahead.
7.0	Turn **left** onto Ervin Rd.
7.8	Turn **right** onto Gruver Rd.
8.4	At the stop sign, turn **left** to continue on Gruver.
8.7	Turn **left** onto Randts Mill Rd.
9.7	When Randts Mill ends at a stop sign, turn **right** onto Ervin Rd.
9.8	When Ervin ends at a stop sign, turn **right** onto Dark Hollow Rd.
10.4	Go **straight** at the stop sign onto Covered Bridge Rd.; the parking area is immediately on your **right**.

Frenchtown

Distance: 8.8 miles
Start: River Road
Frenchtown, N.J.

Like many of these rides, the loop from Frenchtown to Everittstown and back takes you along both town and country roads, but here the contrast is especially strong. Frenchtown itself has a large residential community as well as a mix of shops, galleries, and restaurants, while the rest of the ride passes through farmland and miles of quiet woodland crisscrossed by a maze of small streams.

The ride begins in Frenchtown in the parking area along River Road just south of Bridge Street. To reach it, head toward the river on Bridge Street and make the last left before the bridge. The parking area will be immediately on your left. Bicyclists must watch out for traffic during the short stretch of the ride in Frenchtown. Once you leave town, however, you'll find hardly any traffic at all.

At the beginning of Creek Road, you'll find a Frenchtown Borough park with picnic tables and playground equipment. Though Creek Road has always been passable by bicycle, it was closed to automobile traffic for a few years after a storm took out a guard rail and part of the road. It has since been repaired and reopened, but it continues to be a little rough. The first part is narrow and unpaved as it travels through the woods beside Nishisakawick Creek; the scenery is beautiful, although this stretch of road has a tendency to develop some crater-sized potholes. Eventually, you'll emerge into open farmland and turn toward Everittstown, a country crossroads town set in the midst of rolling fields. On the way, you'll encounter two significant uphill climbs on Route 519. From Everittstown, the route returns to Frenchtown. The last mile into town on Route 513 is downhill, the last half mile steeply so, so ride carefully.

To make the ride a little longer, or if the River Road parking area is full, you can park off Route 29 south of Frenchtown at the Kingwood Township Angler's Access. Leave your car there and ride your bike on the canal path to Frenchtown; it's about a mile north. You'll come into town at the River Road parking area, and you can follow the step-by-step directions from there.

Frenchtown is located about 15 miles north of Lambertville on Route 29. There's a bridge across the river here, so you can come up the New Jersey side or take Route 32 north from New Hope and cross over at Uhlerstown. Either way has its advantages. Route 29 is wider, straighter, less prone to potholes, and faster, but Route 32 is probably more scenic. Consider stopping on the way for a walk across the pedestrian bridge over the Delaware River from the Bull's Island Recreation Area in New Jersey to Lumberville, Pa. (See more about this area in the chapter on Lumberville on page 22.)

Good to know:

Freeman's Bicycle Shop, 52 Bridge St., Frenchtown, (908) 996-7712. A good bike shop right on the route, with bike rentals available.

Jack's Pizzeria, 48 Bridge St., Frenchtown, (908) 996-2511. Your basic small pizzeria; not much on atmosphere, but always good when you're hungry.

Race Street, an interesting row of galleries and restaurants on the short stretch of this street between Kingwood Ave. (Route 12) and Route 29.

Bridge Cafe, 8 Bridge St., Frenchtown, (908) 996-6040. An interesting casual restaurant located next to the River Road parking area in a former train station. It has a glassed-in dining room with a fine view of the river and the bridge.

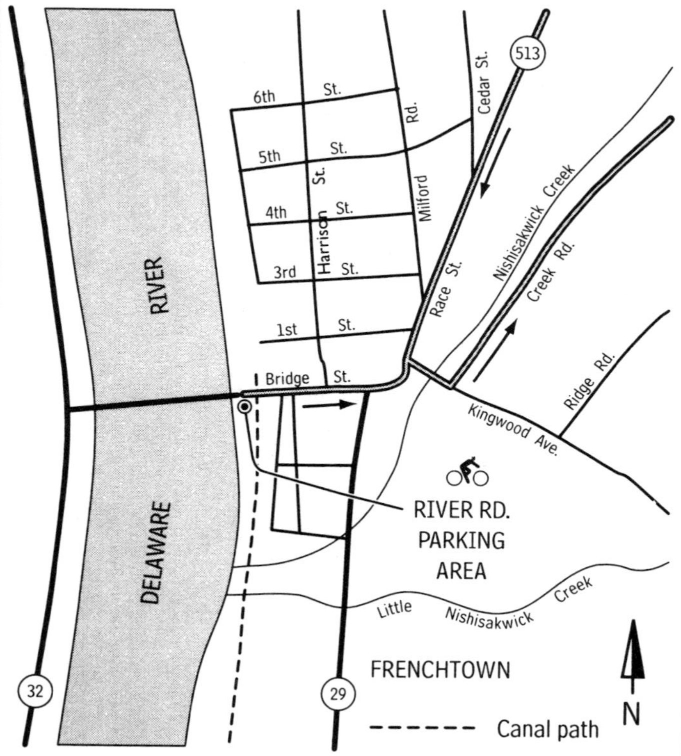

Frenchtown

🚲 Start at the parking area on River Road just south of Bridge St. Turn **right** onto Bridge St. (After the intersection with Route 29, follow the road as it bends sharply to the left and becomes Race St.)

0.1 At the blinking yellow light, turn **right** onto Kingwood Ave. (Route 12). Immediately cross a small creek.

0.2 Just after the creek, turn **left** onto Creek Rd.

(Continued on next page)

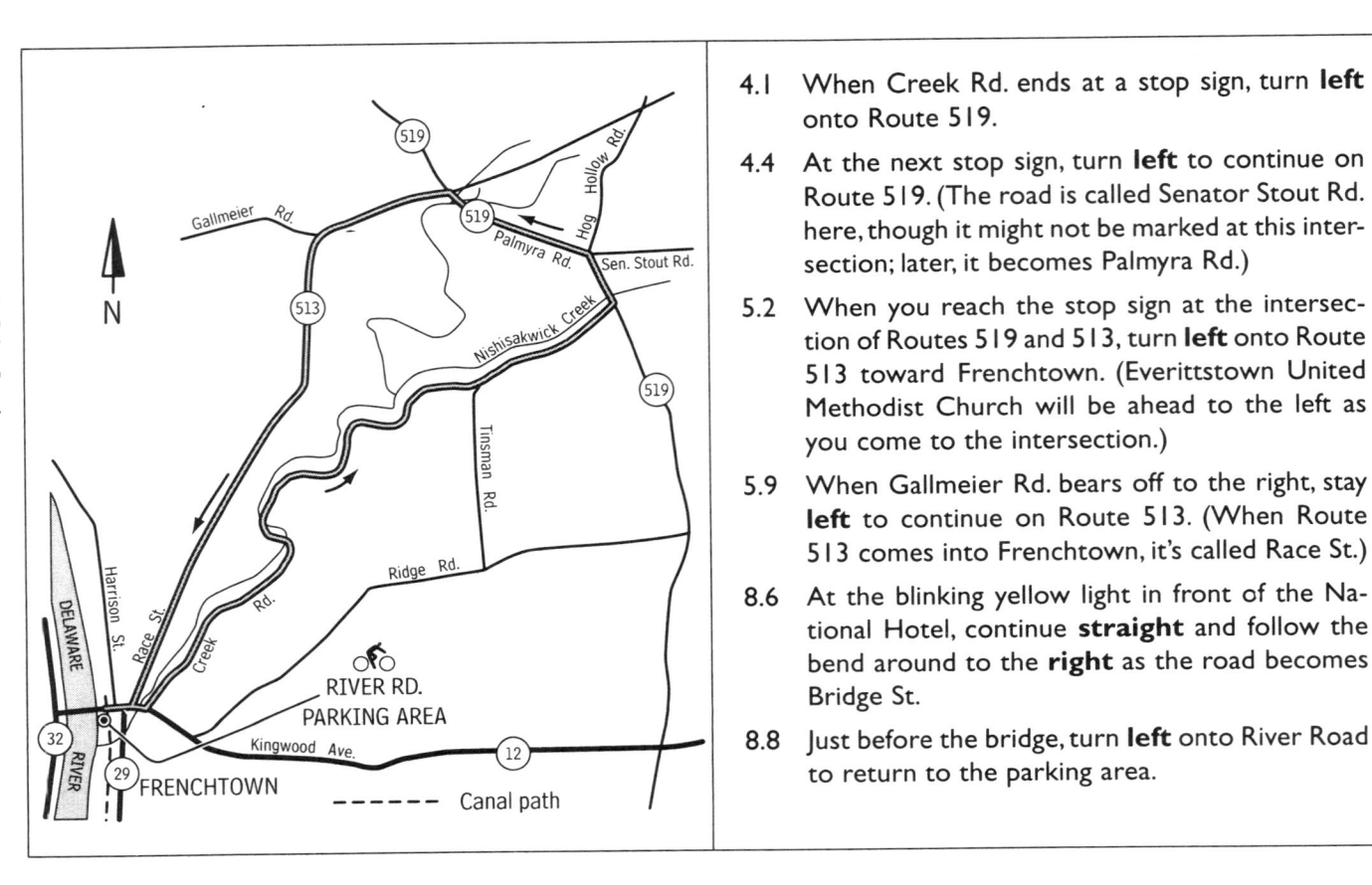

4.1 When Creek Rd. ends at a stop sign, turn **left** onto Route 519.

4.4 At the next stop sign, turn **left** to continue on Route 519. (The road is called Senator Stout Rd. here, though it might not be marked at this intersection; later, it becomes Palmyra Rd.)

5.2 When you reach the stop sign at the intersection of Routes 519 and 513, turn **left** onto Route 513 toward Frenchtown. (Everittstown United Methodist Church will be ahead to the left as you come to the intersection.)

5.9 When Gallmeier Rd. bears off to the right, stay **left** to continue on Route 513. (When Route 513 comes into Frenchtown, it's called Race St.)

8.6 At the blinking yellow light in front of the National Hotel, continue **straight** and follow the bend around to the **right** as the road becomes Bridge St.

8.8 Just before the bridge, turn **left** onto River Road to return to the parking area.

Buckingham Mountain

Distance: 15.0 miles
Start: Holicong Park
Route 202
Buckingham, Pa.

As more and more Bucks County farms sprout development houses instead of corn, the laments about the area's lost beauty grow louder. It's true that some parts of the county are looking increasingly suburban, but the good news is that there are still many isolated pockets where the wonderful scenery this area has been known for continues more or less unspoiled.

The area around Buckingham Mountain is definitely one of those places.

This trip around the mountain has a couple of long hills, but much of the way it is nearly level or gently rolling. It also includes two crossings of busy Route 413 at intersections without traffic lights, so you might want to take this ride early on a weekend morning when there isn't much traffic.

The route begins about six miles from New Hope at Buckingham Township's Holicong Park, located on Route 202 just west of Holicong Road. The park has sports fields, a playground, a picnic pavilion, and rest rooms. A back exit takes you from the recreation area to Holicong Road, and that is where you'll start the ride.

The first part of the route passes large houses and farmland, including large fields where beautiful horses roam. Byecroft Road, which leads from Upper Mountain Road to Route 202, is a detour to nowhere, but it makes a beautiful side trip if you'd like to extend the ride. When you reach Street Road you'll find a development ahead on your left; it's not the most beautiful site on this route, but you'll be turning toward more rural vistas. Lower Mountain Road takes you through the woods at the base of Buckingham Mountain; there's a good view of farms and hills off to the left as you approach Route 413 (also called Durham Road).

On the far side of Route 413, you'll climb a hill into Forest Grove, a lovely little town with an unhurried country feeling. Then it's back out into open farmland, with a view of Buckingham Mountain to your left as you ride along. Keep an eye out for the turn onto New Hope Road, which could pass for a long driveway leading off through the fields on the left.

Once you cross Durham Road you'll be back in the woods again. You pass Holicong Road a number of times on this trip, the final crossing coming on New Hope Road as you approach Pineville Road. (It is possible to turn left on Holicong Road here and cross straight over the spine of Buckingham Mountain, but this is a tough hill suitable only for cyclists who love punishment. There isn't as much of a view as you might expect at the top, where you'll find the Mount Gilead A.M.E. church, a small stone building beside an old graveyard, which did service in the nineteenth century as a stop on the Underground Railroad.) After Holicong, the last part of New Hope Road before Pineville Road is unpaved.

The final part of the ride retraces the route along Street Road, Upper Mountain Road, and Holicong Road back to the park.

La Vecchia Cucina is the only restaurant directly on the route, but at several shopping centers nearby you'll find both sit-down restaurants and delis that sell takeout food. Buckingham Green is located on Route 202 about a quarter mile west of Holicong Park; Peddler's Village and Hollyberry Square are also on Route 202 about a mile in the other direction.

Good to know:

Deli on the Green, Buckingham Green, Route 202, Buckingham, (215) 794-5799. Takeout food and drinks.

Evolution Pro Bike and Ski Shop, Routes 413 & 202, Buckingham, (215) 794-9600. A bike shop located about a mile west of the start of the ride.

Lahaska Deli, Hollyberry Square, Route 202, Lahaska, (215) 794-8055. Takeout food and drinks.

La Vecchia Cucina, Route 413 and Lower Mountain Rd., Buckingham, (215) 794-7500. Homemade breads and pastas, pizzas from a woodburning oven. Outdoor and indoor tables. The kind of place where reservations are required for dinner on weekends; brunch served Saturdays and Sundays from 8 A.M. to noon.

Peddler's Village, Route 202, Lahaska, (215) 794-4000. More than 70 shops and 8 restaurants nestled in a landscaped little town of their own, with brick walkways and gardens and a real carousel. It's commercial, but everything in the Village is done so well that it's hard to resist its charms. It's located about a mile east of the start of the ride.

Buckingham Mountain

- 🚴 At the Holicong Rd. exit from Holicong Park, turn **right** onto Holicong Rd.
- 0.6 Turn **left** onto Upper Mountain Rd.
- 1.8 At the stop sign, turn **right** onto Street Rd.
- 2.7 At a five-way intersection, make the sharp **right** onto Lower Mountain Rd.
- 4.1 At the four-way stop, cross Holicong Rd. and continue **straight** on Lower Mountain Rd.
- 5.3 At the stop sign, **carefully** cross Route 413 (Durham Rd.) and continue **straight** on Lower Mountain Rd.
- 6.8 At the stop sign in the center of Forest Grove, turn **left** onto Forest Grove Rd.
- 8.0 Turn **left** onto New Hope Rd.
- 9.7 At the stop sign, **carefully** cross Route 413 (also known as Durham Rd.) and continue **straight** on New Hope.

44 ◆ The Back Roads Bike Book

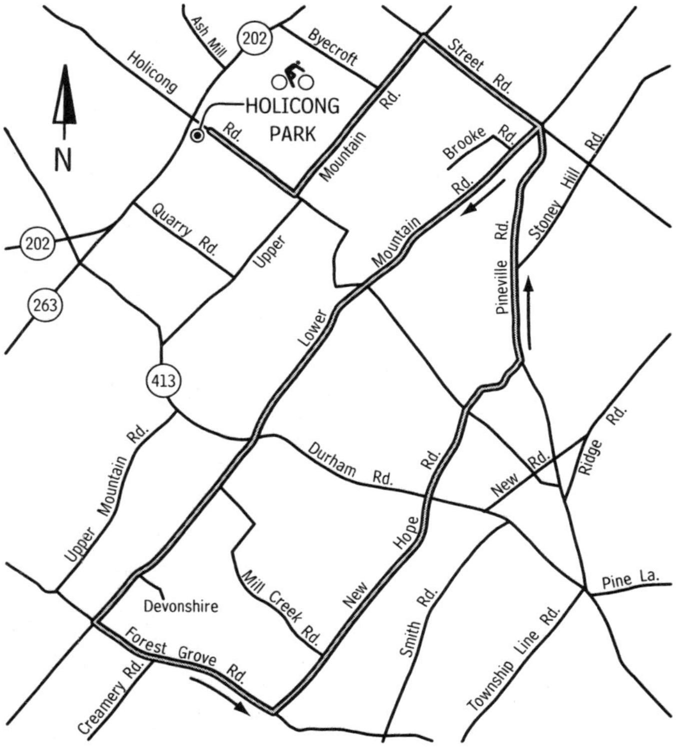

10.8 When New Hope ends at a stop sign, turn **left** onto Pineville Rd.
12.2 At the stop sign, turn **left** onto Street Rd.
13.1 Turn **left** onto Upper Mountain.
14.4 At the stop sign, turn **right** onto Holicong.
15.0 At the entrance to Holicong Park, turn **left** to return to the parking area.

Buckingham Mountain ◆ 45

Pidcock Creek

Distance: 11.0 miles
Start: Bowman's Hill Wildflower Preserve
Route 32
Solebury Township, Pa.

This is a ride with a view of the mountains, such as they are in this area. Bowman's Hill rises above the Delaware River just south of Aquetong Road near the Bowman's Hill Wildflower Preserve, and Jericho Mountain lies nearby. Fortunately, looking at these elevations doesn't have to mean cycling up them—the route skirts carefully around the big hills to stay on fairly level ground.

The ride officially begins at the intersection of Route 32 and Aquetong Road, about two and a half miles south of New Hope. There are several places where you can park your car nearby. Most obvious is the state park itself; Bowman's Hill and the land around it are part of the northern extension of Pennsylvania's Washington Crossing Historic Park. If you leave your car in the parking area near the river and ride back up the park road to cross Route 32 at the foot of Aquetong Road, you can avoid riding on Route 32 at all—a definite advantage. If you park across Route 32 near the wildflower preserve, you'll have only a short ride along Route 32 to Aquetong. The disadvantage of using either of these areas is that it'll cost you; you'll have to plunk four quarters into a mechanized guard gate to get in. In addition, the park is closed on Mondays. You can park for

A farm along Ridge Road

free in a small cleared area on the east side of Route 32 just south of the wildflower preserve, the disadvantage being that you must ride farther on Route 32, which is narrow and carries a lot of traffic.

Once you start up Aquetong Road, however, you'll leave most of that traffic behind. You'll travel through woodlands near Pidcock Creek, then pass the dairy farms along Ridge Road. The pretty view of the ridge makes this a wonderful ride to take in the fall when the leaves are turning. When you reach Route 413, another busy road, you might want to get off your bike and walk along the shoulder in front of the Pineville Tavern for the short distance from Pineville Road to Pine Lane.

On the way back, you'll ride through the Van Sant Covered Bridge, built in 1875 across Pidcock Creek. After that, it's best to retrace the start of the ride along Aquetong Road. As an alternative, it's possible to skip the covered bridge and continue straight on Lurgan Road to Route 32, where you turn left to return to the start of the ride. Because of the traffic on Route 32, however, this route is not recommended.

Take a look around the park before you leave the area. The 80-acre Bowman's Hill Wildflower Preserve, which was founded to preserve and display Pennsylvania's native plants, includes 26 walking trails as well as a preserve building with nature displays, a gift shop, and a bird observation area. The park continues along the river on the other side of Route 32, where there are more picnic areas and a section with the graves of Continental soldiers who died while Washington's troops were camped in the area.

Just south of the wildflower preserve in another section of the park is Bowman's Hill Tower, a 110-foot observation tower atop a 380-foot hill, which is open to the public every day except Mondays in spring, summer, and fall. The hill is said to have been used by Washington's men to observe British troop movements across the river before Washington's famous crossing. The tower, which offers a fantastic view of the surrounding countryside, was built as a memorial. The entrance to the tower is on Lurgan Road about three-quarters of a mile from Route 32. Bikes are prohibited from the extremely steep road up to the tower, so you'll have to give in and drive if you want to enjoy the panoramic view. (A small fee is charged.)

You won't find many stores or restaurants along this route, so consider bringing a picnic and enjoying it in one of the picnic areas in the park when you are done.

Good to know:

Sandy's Country Store, Route 413, Pineville, (215) 598-3523. In the same building as the Pineville Post Office. This store specializes in gifts and foods from Scotland. You can get a cold drink and takeout food, as long as you're happy with a sausage roll or some other typically Scottish fare.

Bowman's Hill Wildflower Preserve, Route 32, Solebury Township, (215) 862-2924.

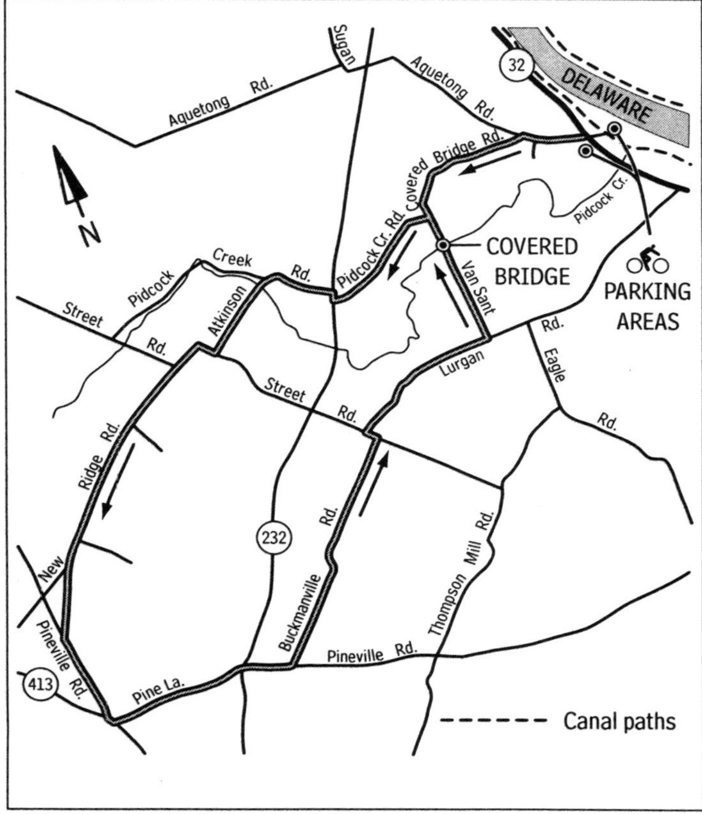

Pidcock Creek

- Start at the intersection of Route 32 and Aquetong Rd. Ride west on Aquetong (away from the river).
- 0.3 Turn **left** onto Covered Bridge Rd., across from the Thompson Memorial Church.
- 1.2 Turn **right** onto Pidcock Creek Rd.
- 2.0 Turn **right** onto Windy Bush Rd. (Route 232) and immediately turn **left** to continue on Pidcock Creek Rd.
- 2.4 When Pidcock Creek Rd. goes off to the right, go **straight** onto Atkinson Rd.
- 2.9 Turn **right** onto Street Rd.
- 3.3 When Street Rd. turns to the right, go **straight** onto Ridge Rd.
- 4.5 When New Rd. goes off to the right, stay **left** to continue on Ridge.
- 4.9 When Ridge ends at a stop sign, turn **left** onto Pineville Rd.

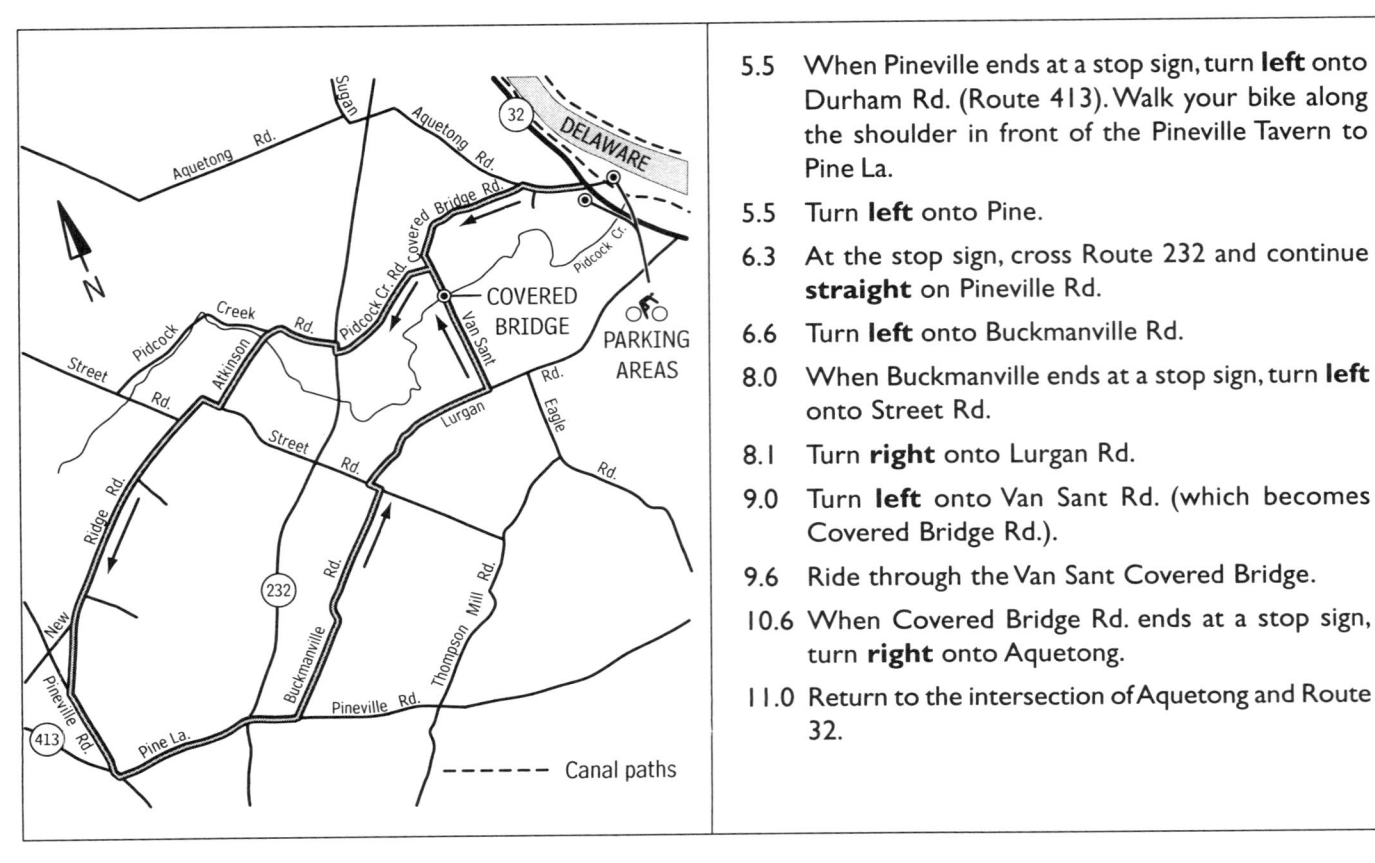

5.5	When Pineville ends at a stop sign, turn **left** onto Durham Rd. (Route 413). Walk your bike along the shoulder in front of the Pineville Tavern to Pine La.
5.5	Turn **left** onto Pine.
6.3	At the stop sign, cross Route 232 and continue **straight** on Pineville Rd.
6.6	Turn **left** onto Buckmanville Rd.
8.0	When Buckmanville ends at a stop sign, turn **left** onto Street Rd.
8.1	Turn **right** onto Lurgan Rd.
9.0	Turn **left** onto Van Sant Rd. (which becomes Covered Bridge Rd.).
9.6	Ride through the Van Sant Covered Bridge.
10.6	When Covered Bridge Rd. ends at a stop sign, turn **right** onto Aquetong.
11.0	Return to the intersection of Aquetong and Route 32.

Washington Crossing

Distance: 13.4 miles
Start: Belle Mountain Ski Area
Valley Rd.
Hopewell Township, N.J.

You might think a bike ride that begins at a ski area would include a few hills—and you'd be right. This is one of the more challenging rides in the book, although it's also one of the most interesting. The route begins at the Belle Mountain Ski Area in Mercer County and takes you along the Delaware & Raritan Canal, into New Jersey's Washington Crossing State Park, and back through Hopewell Township.

You can park your car in the lot for the ski area on Valley Road, about two-tenths of a mile from Route 29. The intersection is well marked with signs for Belle Mountain and the Howell Living History Farm. The ride begins with a short downhill back to Route 29, where you'll cross over to the canal towpath. This is a busy road, so pay careful attention to traffic as you cross. You might not see the entrance to the canal right away; it's to your left as you cross, and it looks like an overgrown path to nowhere. As you approach the gate, however, you'll see a sign for the Delaware & Raritan Canal. The path to the canal is rocky and somewhat steep, so you might want to walk your bike down to the bottom. Cross the bridge over the canal and turn left on the path. From there you'll ride between the canal and the river to Titusville, where you'll pick up River Road.

Titusville is unique. It has the feeling of a small New England town perched above the river. When the town ends you'll actually be riding into Washington Crossing State Park, which commemorates George Washington's crossing of the ice-choked Delaware River on Christmas Day, 1776, after which he marched into Trenton and surprised the Hessians, changing the course of the Revolutionary War. Here you'll find rest rooms, picnic tables, and lots of benches with a view of the spot where Washington is said to have crossed. (History buffs interested in a short detour can walk across the bridge over the Delaware to visit the Memorial Center or historical buildings in Pennsylvania's Washington Crossing Historic Park.)

Cross the pedestrian bridge over Route 29 into the main part of the park, where you can stop to see the Visitor Center and the park's collection of historic buildings. The ride through the park is through shaded woodland, and there's rarely much traffic in the areas where automobiles are allowed. Eventually, you'll leave the park to ride around it on Route 546 and Bear Tavern Rd., which is also known as Trenton-Harbourton Rd. and Harbourton-Rocktown Rd. Both of these roads carry a fair amount of traffic, but ample shoulders provide room for bicyclists, too.

From the river up to the turn onto Valley Road, the route is rolling but basically uphill. In the last part of the ride, along Valley and Pleasant Valley roads, you'll be passing mostly through farmland on roads that have a few hills but basically take you downhill again. Pleasant Valley offers a nice panoramic view of the surrounding countryside. On Valley Road, you can stop to visit the Howell farm, which is kept the way a horse-powered farm in this area would have been around 1900. The last uphill ends at Goat Hill Road; from there you can coast back to the parking area at Belle Mountain.

Good to know

Howell Living History Farm, Valley Rd., Titusville, (609) 737-3299. Operated as a local farm would have been circa 1900, with farming or craft programs on weekends; self-guided tour available on other days.

Faherty's on the Delaware, Routes 29 and 546, Washington Crossing, (609) 737-0400. Restaurant located next to the canal at the foot of the pedestrian bridge over Route 29 from the main part of Washington Crossing State Park. Bike rack. Outdoor dining area on deck overlooking the river. Wine & cheese shop with deli.

Washington Crossing State Park, Routes 29 & 546, Washington Crossing, N.J., (609) 737-0623.

Washington Crossing Historic Park, Routes 32 & 532, Washington Crossing, Pa., (215) 493-4076.

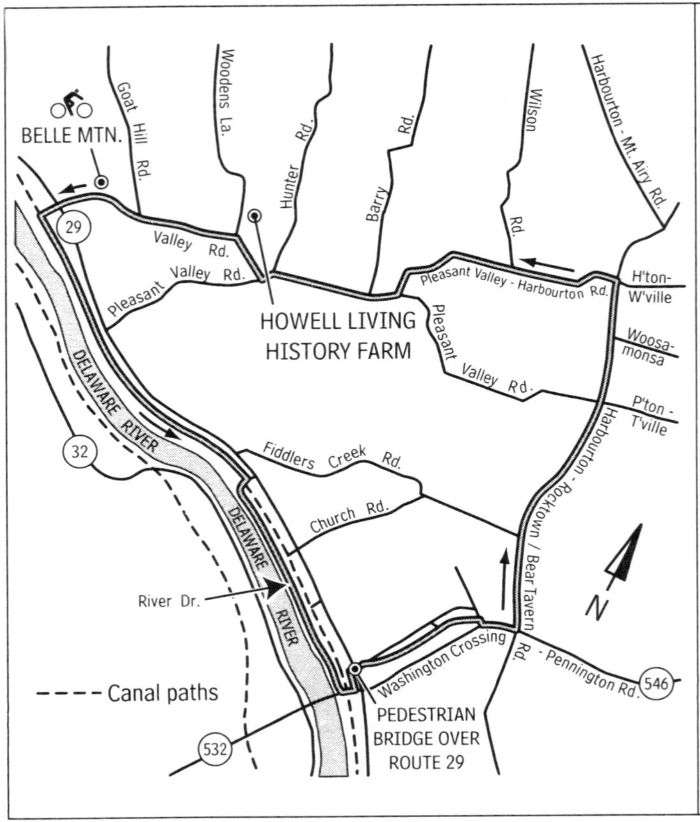

Washington Crossing

🚲 Start at the parking lot across from the Belle Mountain Public Ski Area. Turn **right** from the parking lot onto Valley Rd.

0.2 At the stop sign, cross Route 29 carefully. To the **left** you'll see what looks like an overgrown path with a sign indicating that it's an entrance to the Delaware and Raritan Canal. This trail is somewhat rocky; you might wish to walk your bike to the bottom, where you'll cross the canal and turn **left** on the bike path.

2.8 At the next white bridge over the canal, turn **right** from the bike path onto River Dr.

4.6 When River Dr. ends at a stop sign at Route 546 (next to the bridge across the Delaware), bear **left**. On the **left** just across the canal you'll find a pedestrian bridge across Route 29. When the bridge ends, follow the path through the park. (Both bridge and path are shared with pedestrians, so ride carefully.)

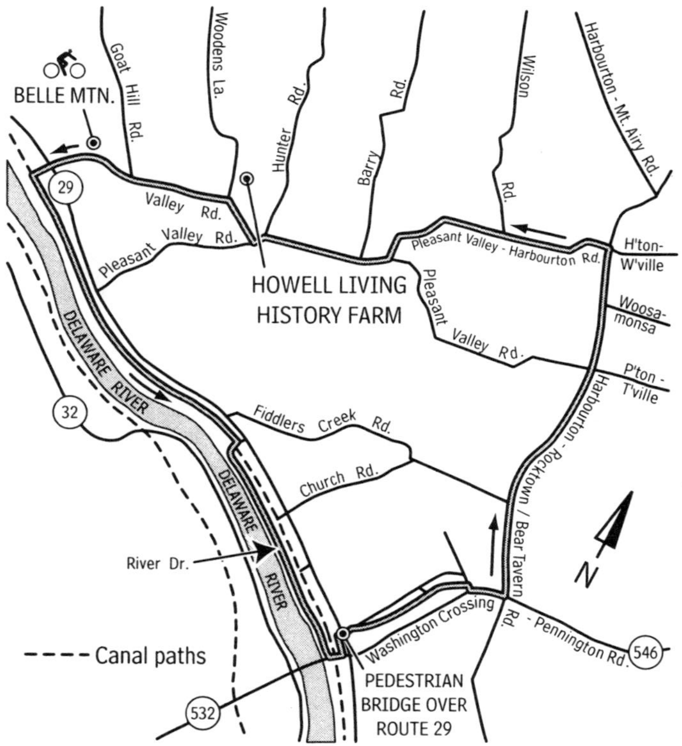

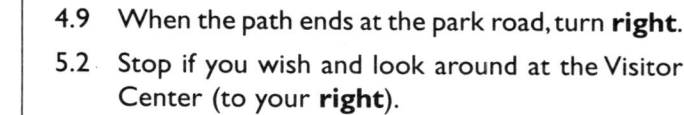

4.9 When the path ends at the park road, turn **right**.
5.2 Stop if you wish and look around at the Visitor Center (to your **right**).
5.5 At the stop sign, turn **right** toward the park exit.
5.7 At the stop sign, turn **left** onto Route 546.
6.3 At the traffic light, turn **left** onto Route 579. (It's also marked Bear Tavern Rd.)
9.1 Turn **left** onto Pleasant Valley-Harbourton Rd. (The sign on the right says Harbourton-Woodsville Rd.)
10.9 At the stop sign, turn **right** onto Pleasant Valley Rd.
11.9 Turn **right** onto Valley Rd.
12.3 Pass the sign for the Howell Living History Farm. Stop if you wish to visit the farm.
13.4 Return to the parking area.

Washington Crossing ◆ 55

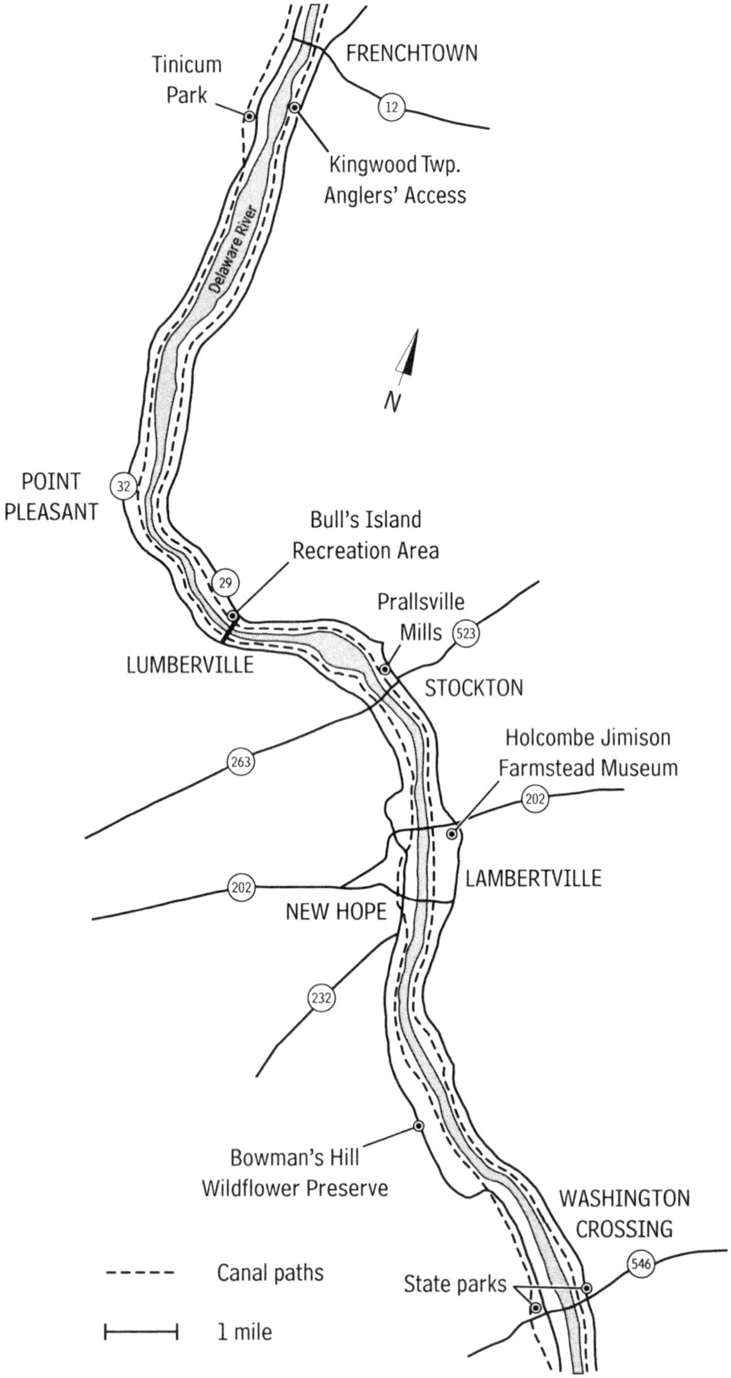
FRENCHTOWN
Tinicum Park
12
Kingwood Twp. Anglers' Access
Delaware River
N
POINT PLEASANT
32
Bull's Island Recreation Area
29
Prallsville Mills
523
LUMBERVILLE
STOCKTON
263
Holcombe Jimison Farmstead Museum
202
LAMBERTVILLE
202
NEW HOPE
232
Bowman's Hill Wildflower Preserve
WASHINGTON CROSSING
546
Canal paths
State parks
1 mile

Riding the canals

If you're determined to do your bicycling on routes that are perfectly flat and absolutely without traffic, go ride the canals along the Delaware River.

New Jersey's Delaware & Raritan Canal and the Delaware Division of the Pennsylvania Canal were built in the nineteenth century to carry coal, building materials, and farm produce to market. Though they've long since outlived that function, they have been turned into state parks with multi-use trails that are extremely popular with bicyclists.

The New Jersey trail is wide and level and is made of hard-packed crushed stone. It is much more pleasant for cycling than the towpath in Pennsylvania, which is grassy and occasionally slopes so severely toward the canal that you must get off your bike and walk. Although authorities in Pennsylvania have promised to construct a new bike path from Morrisville to Uhlerstown, present conditions there require a bike with relatively wide tires, such as a mountain bike.

In New Jersey, the path follows an abandoned railroad right-of-way that runs along the Delaware River. Between Ewing and Lambertville, the trail runs right next to the canal, but north of Stockton there are woods and houses between them. Farther north, past the end of the canal at the Bull's Island Recreation Area, the trail once again runs quite close to the river.

A long-awaited construction project completed during the summer of 1998 brought the path all the way through Lambertville, making it possible to ride straight through from just north of Trenton to Frenchtown. (Cyclists previously had to detour through city streets in Lambertville.) Good places to park for a canal ride include Washington Crossing State Park, the Holcombe Jimison Farmstead Museum, Prallsville Mills, and Bull's Island, an 80-acre state park with picnic areas, camp grounds, easy access to the Delaware, and a pedestrian bridge across to Lumberville on the Pennsylvania side of the river. Parking is also available at the Kingwood Township Angler's Access just south of Frenchtown.

Even though the path in New Jersey is level and smooth and carries no automobile traffic, it is not always good for beginning cyclists who have not mastered riding in a straight line. If you veer off the towpath as it runs along right next to the canal, you risk tumbling into the water. Just south of Lambertville, the ride is especially scenic, but there's a sharp drop to the river bank not far from the edge of the towpath.

This chapter focuses on the New Jersey side of the river because conditions are so much more favorable there for cycling, although there are instructions under the Stockton to Bull's Island section for a loop ride that crosses the river at Lumberville and again at Centre Bridge so you can ride on both sides. (Individual route maps are not provided because it's hard to get lost when you ride out and back in a straight line.)

See the chapters on Washington Crossing, Lambertville, Stockton, Lumberville, and Frenchtown for more listings.

Good to know:

Delaware Canal State Park, (610) 982-5560. A 60-mile park running the length of the Delaware Canal in Pennsylvania.

Delaware & Raritan Canal State Park, (732) 873-3050. An 80-mile park running beside the canal from Milford to Trenton to New Brunswick in New Jersey.

The former Stockton station now houses shops beside the bike path

Bull's Island to Frenchtown

8 miles one way

The canal ends at Bull's Island, so from here north the trail is the only thing between Route 29 and the river. Route 29 has a wide, smooth shoulder, and many cyclists enjoy making a loop ride going out along the path and back via the road. It's a level and very pretty ride, but somewhat isolated until you arrive in Frenchtown.

A cyclist on the canal path south of Lambertville

Washington Crossing to Lambertville

7 miles one way

Washington Crossing State Park is a good place to leave your car while you ride the canal path into Lambertville, where you can take a break to have lunch and look around the shops before you ride back. Leave your car in the parking area located on River Drive near the bridge to Pennsylvania.

You'll know you've arrived in Lambertville when you reach the intersection with Bridge Street, right across the canal from the Lambertville Station Restaurant.

For a shorter ride, you can park at the Holcombe Jimison Farmstead about a mile north of Bridge Street or in a small parking area beside the canal about two miles south. To reach it from Route 29, cross the white bridge over the canal directly across from Old River Road, which is just south of the Rooster's Coop lighting store.

You'll find some on-street parking in Lambertville itself, but most of the spaces near the center of town are metered.

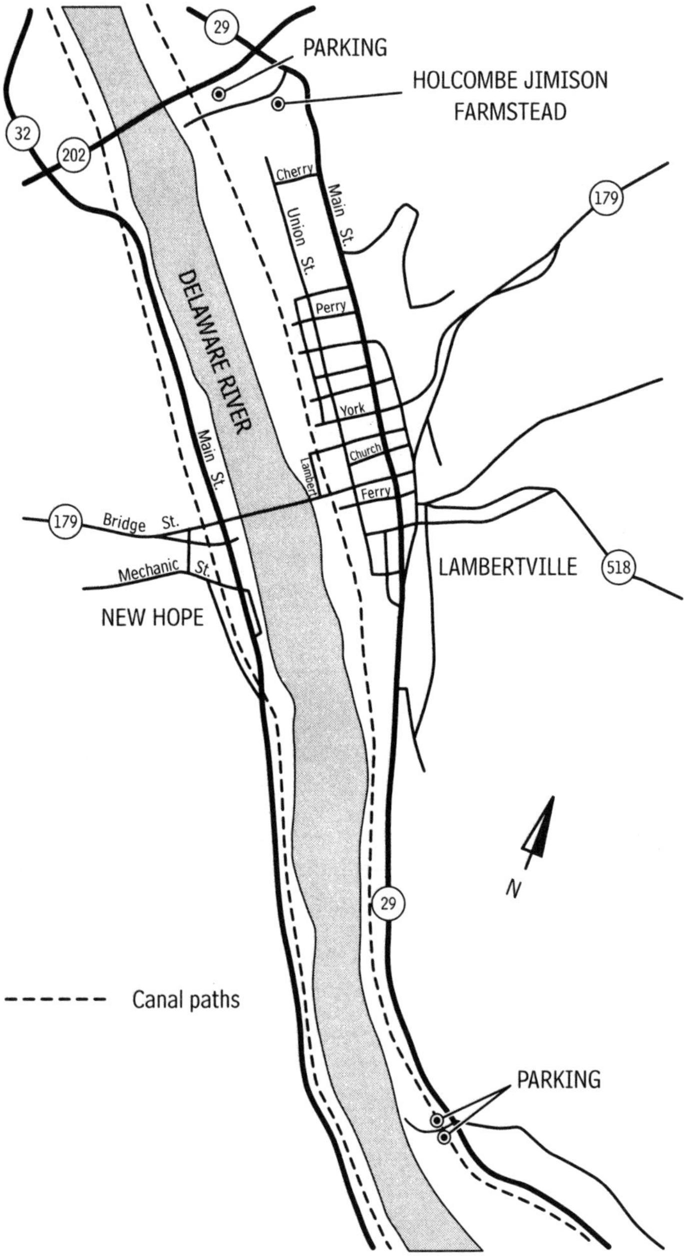
29
PARKING
HOLCOMBE JIMISON
FARMSTEAD
32
202
Cherry
Main St.
Union St.
179
DELAWARE RIVER
Perry
York
Church
Lambert
Ferry
Main St.
179
Bridge St.
Mechanic St.
NEW HOPE
LAMBERTVILLE
518
N
29
Canal paths
PARKING

Stockton to Bull's Island

3 miles one way

This stretch of the Delaware & Raritan trail in New Jersey is especially good for young riders because there's little danger of riding off the path here. You can park on the street in Lumberville, at the Bull's Island Recreation Area, or at Prallsville Mills. You can also use the parking area behind the Holcombe Jimison Farmstead just south of Route 202 in Lambertville, riding north to Stockton from there.

Using these directions, which begin in Lumberville, you can make a loop ride that includes a stretch of the canal in Pennsylvania.

0.0 Start at the pedestrian bridge on Route 32 in Lumberville. Walk your bike across the bridge into the Bull's Island Recreation Area and ride straight ahead on the park road.

0.3 Just before Route 29, turn **right** on the bike trail and ride south toward Stockton.

1.5 Walk your bike over the bridge so your wheels won't get caught between the planks.

3.1 Cross another stream on a wide bridge. Prallsville Mills is to your left; on your right, there's a good view of the Delaware River.

3.5 Turn **right** on Bridge St. in Stockton (it's the second road the path intersects after Prallsville Mills). Ride to the bridge over the Delaware River and walk your bike across.

3.9 At the end of the bridge, carry your bike down the steps to the canal towpath and ride north toward Lumberville.

7.3 Ride under the pedestrian bridge that crosses to Bull's Island.

Planning longer rides

The bike tours included in this book are all relatively short, but cyclists who prefer to ride farther can easily join two or more of the tours together to create a longer ride. Here are some examples:

1. Start the New Hope ride. When you reach Bridge Street in New Hope near the end of the ride, turn left and walk your bike across the bridge to Lambertville. Ride ahead to the Delaware & Raritan Canal and turn right on the bike path. Take the canal path south to Titusville and pick up the Washington Crossing ride. When you reach the parking lot across from Belle Mountain, continue straight ahead to Route 29. Follow the directions to cross Route 29 and go down to the canal path, but turn right to return to Lambertville. When you reach Bridge Street, turn left and ride to the bridge. Walk your bike across to New Hope and finish the New Hope ride.

2. Start the Lambertville ride. When you return to the parking area behind the Holcombe Jimison Farmstead, turn right on the canal bike path and head north to Stockton. Cross Bridge Street on the path and continue to Prallsville Mills. When you reach the mills, begin the Rosemont ride. After you return to Prallsville Mills, follow

the canal bike path back to the parking area behind the Holcombe Jimison Farmstead.

3. Take the Rosemont ride. When you return to the parking area at Prallsville Mills, turn right on the canal bike path to head north to the Bull's Island Recreation Area. Cross the pedestrian bridge to Lumberville and take the Lumberville ride. At the end of that route, cross the bridge back to the Bull's Island Recreation Area and follow the canal path or Route 29 south to return to the Prallsville Mills.

4. Take the Lumberville ride. At the end of the route, cross the pedestrian bridge to the Bull's Island Recreation Area and begin the Tumble Falls ride. When you return to the Bull's Island Recreation area, cross the pedestrian bridge over the Delaware River to return to Lumberville.

5. Park at the Bull's Island Recreation Area. Ride the canal bike path or Route 29 north to Frenchtown. Take the Frenchtown ride. Near the end of the route, turn left on Route 29 and ride south as far as Warsaw Road. Turn left on Warsaw Road to pick up the Tumble Falls ride, which ends back at the Bull's Island Recreation Area.

Places to stay

A pleasant ride along scenic back roads, a little shopping, a delicious dinner out, all capped off with a good night's sleep at a cozy country inn—what cycling enthusiast could think of a better way to spend a day?

The area around New Hope and Lambertville is justly popular with tourists, and there are far too many wonderful places to stay to include them all. These listings are not comprehensive, but they will give you some idea of what's available. The agencies included at the bottom of the list can help you plan a visit to the area.

1740 House, River Road, Lumberville PA 18933, (215) 297-5661, fax (215) 297-5243. All 24 rooms have private bath, a terrace or balcony, and A/C. Most have a king-size bed and a picture window overlooking the Delaware River. Buffet breakfast served in an enclosed brick terrace on the riverfront.

Aaron Burr House Inn, 80 W. Bridge St. (corner Chestnut Street), New Hope PA 18938, tel/fax (215) 862-2570. Gracious vintage Victorian B&B, located steps from the village center and the Delaware Canal and River. 3 ♦ rated by AAA. A member of the Wedgwood Collection of Inns. Close to the NYC bus, all private baths, A/C,

The classic view from New Hope: Lambertville and the river

and even a barn to store your bicycles. Some rooms have canopy beds and fireplaces. Web site: www.new-hope-inn.com; e-mail: stay@new-hope-inn.com.

Evermay on-the-Delaware, P.O. Box 60, 889 River Rd., Erwinna PA 18920, (610) 294-9100, fax (610) 294-8249. An elegant Victorian house hotel, listed on the National Register of Historic Places, located on 25 acres of pastures, woodlands, and gardens. This very highly rated "intimate inn" has 16 rooms, all with private bath. An award-winning six-course dinner is served Friday, Saturday, and Sunday.

Hunterdon House, 12 Bridge St., Frenchtown NJ 08825, (908) 996-3632, fax (908) 996-0942. Italianate Victorian B&B inn, circa 1864, located one half block from the Delaware River in historic Frenchtown. Seven guest bedrooms with private bathrooms and furnished with period antiques. Full menu breakfast served every morning. Easy access to off-road bike paths in NJ and PA.

Inn at Lambertville Station, 11 Bridge St., Lambertville NJ 08530, (609) 397-4400, fax (609) 397-9744. Modern hotel with the gracious feeling of an older establishment. Forty-five rooms with river view, antiques, continental breakfast included, central location near the canal bike path, covered bike storage. Restaurant serving 365 days.

Tattersall Inn, P.O. Box 569, River & Cafferty rds., Point Pleasant PA 18950, (215) 297-8233, (800) 297-4988, fax (215) 297-5093. Historic 18th-century Stover Mansion in village setting, with spacious rooms, some with fireplaces, private bath, A/C, beamed-ceiling common room with walk-in fireplace available for relaxation. Full breakfast, mid-week discount, 3 ♦ rated by AAA.

Woolverton Inn, 6 Woolverton Rd., Stockton NJ 08559, (609) 397-4936, (888) AN-INN-4U. Guests enjoy sipping wine by the fireplace in their room, or slipping into a cozy terrycloth robe after a Jacuzzi. Relaxed yet attentive atmosphere, full country candlelight breakfast, classic country setting. Amenities include A/C, private baths, soft towels, antiques, afternoon refreshments, bike storage. Minutes from numerous scenic bike rides. Biking packages include *The Back Roads Bike Book*, lunch at a local bistro.

Bucks County Conference and Visitors Bureau, 152 Swamp Rd., Doylestown PA 18901, (215) 345-4552, (800) 836-2825, fax (215) 345-4967. Web site: www.buckscountycvb.org; e-mail: bctc@bccvb.org

Chamber of Commerce of the Lambertville Area, 4 S. Union St., Lambertville NJ 08530, (609) 397-0055.

New Hope Borough Information Center, South Main and Mechanic sts., New Hope, (215) 862-5880.

Local biking on the Internet

The Internet is a good resource for information about bicycling, with a growing number of sites devoted to riding in Pennsylvania and New Jersey. Just one problem: Things tend to change so quickly that any attempt to publish the addresses of pertinent Web sites in a book is likely to include some links that were out of date before it could be printed.

For that reason, we suggest linking to our homepage on the World Wide Web:

Bike New Hope
http://www.voicenet.com/~ckerr

We'll be using the site to provide useful—and up-to-date—information about bicycling near Lambertville and New Hope.

Keep in touch

Do you have a favorite back roads bike ride of your own? Was there anything you especially liked (or didn't like) about one of the rides in this book? We'd like to know what you think. You can send a letter or e-mail.

Please share your thoughts about these routes. Tell us if road conditions have changed, or if you have corrections to any of the directions or listings. Let us know if you discovered any noteworthy things to do not mentioned in this book.

Also, tell us about your own favorite bicycling routes. (They don't have to be in Bucks County.) Rides suggested by readers may be included in future editions of this or other bicycle tour books.

Please send your comments and suggestions to:

Freewheeling Press
P.O. Box 540
Lahaska PA 18931

You can also reach us via e-mail:
ckerr@voicenet.com

You can find useful information about bicycling in Bucks County and keep up with what's happening here at Freewheeling Press by visiting our Web site:

Bike New Hope
http://www.voicenet.com/~ckerr

Buy a book

It's easy to order one of Freewheeling Press's acclaimed bicycle tour books by mail. Use this form to get a copy of this book for a friend, or treat yourself to our guide to bicycling in Bucks County. *Back Roads Bicycling in Bucks County, Pa.* features rides ranging in length from 7.9 to 47.1 miles and includes information on bike paths and local bicycling clubs.

Name: _____

Address: _____

_____

Telephone: _____

No.	Title	Price	Total
	Back Roads Bicycling in Bucks County, Pa.	$12.95	
	The Back Roads Bike Book	$12.95	
Send to: **Freewheeling Press** **PO Box 540** **Lahaska PA 18931**	Subtotal		
	Shipping ($2 per book)		
	Pa. residents add 6% tax		
	Grand total		
	Make check payable to Freewheeling Press		